FROM TIMBUKTU TO THE MISSISSIPPI DELTA

How West African Standards of Aesthetics Have Shaped the Music of the Delta Blues

By Dr. Pascal Bokar Thiam
University of San Francisco

Foreword by
NEA Jazz Master, Composer & Pianist
Randy Weston

cognella™
San Diego, CA

Bassim Hamadeh, CEO and Publisher
Michael Simpson, Vice President of Acquisitions
Jamie Giganti, Managing Editor
Miguel Macias, Graphic Designer
Kristina Stolte, Acquisitions Editor
Michelle Piehl, Project Editor
Alexa Lucido, Licensing Coordinator

First published in the United States of America in 2015 by Cognella, Inc.

Trademark Notice: Product or corporate names may be trademarks or registered trademarks, and are used only for identification and explanation without intent to infringe.

Printed in the United States of America

ISBN: 978-1-63487-105-1(pbk) / 978-1-63487-106-8 (br) / 978-1-63487-267-6 (hc)

www.cognella.com 800.200.3908

Foreword

The Music is so varied that we still have no real idea what African music is.

I do know this, though: When an African touches an instrument, whether that African is an extension like Louis Armstrong or a master healer from Morocco or Mississippi, that instrument becomes an African instrument.

When a person is touched by African music, from his skin to his soul, that person has become Africanized. Perhaps this is the true meaning of universal: something foreign that reminds you of your deepest self.

Dr. Thiam has made a major contribution and this book should be in every school and home.

Peace and Blessings,

Randy Weston
Composer & Pianist
NEA Jazz Master

Reviews

In this beautifully crafted and timely book about music, Dr. Pascal Bokar Thiam guides us straight to the serious questions of the origin of Jazz and Blues throughout a long journey across West Africa. This book persuasively describes the contributions of West Africans in both classical and modern music, and provides valuable information about the antecedents, the culture, the personalities, the misfortune and triumphs of both West African and black American music alike. This book is a must read for those who care not only about music, but are also interested in social justice, colonization and slavery.

Magueye Seck, Ph.D.
Professor of Sociology
Curry College, Massachusetts

Much of currently available scholarship continues to spin the wise old tale of blues and jazz that goes something along the lines of "… up the river from New Orleans …", which is indeed a romantic and Americanized notion. But the true roots of the blues go back thousands of years before that. Pascal Bokar Thiam, himself a working musician in addition to his scholarly pursuits, journeys us back to root sources, visiting ancient string, voice and cultural traditions of Africa that shed revealing light on the birth of the blues. The photos in this book alone are worth the exploration. *From Timbuktu to the Mississippi Delta* is an invaluable addition to studies of the true roots of what the sage Art Ensemble of Chicago always referred to as "Great Black Music, ancient to the future."

Willard Jenkins
Arranger *African Rhythms*,
the autobiography of NEA Jazz Master Randy Weston
www.openskyjazz.com

From Timbuktu to the Mississippi Delta makes the most compelling argument for the African roots of blues and jazz. Dr. Pascal Bokar Thiam not only documents the trans-Atlantic crossings of West African musical practices, but he demonstrates that an entire aesthetic philosophy survived the Middle Passage. This book ought to be mandatory reading for anyone remotely interested in modern music and its ancient lineage.

Robin D. G. Kelley, PhD
Author of *Thelonious Monk: The Life and Times of an American Original (2009)*
Professor of American Studies and Ethnicity,
University of Southern California, Los Angeles

From left to right: **Dr. Pascal Bokar Thiam, Toumani Diabate, and Dr. Yassine Badian-Kouyate**

Grandfather Mamadou Lamine Thiam, administrator during
colonial times in Senegal, patriarch of the Thiam Clan with uncles
Doudou and Badou Thiam

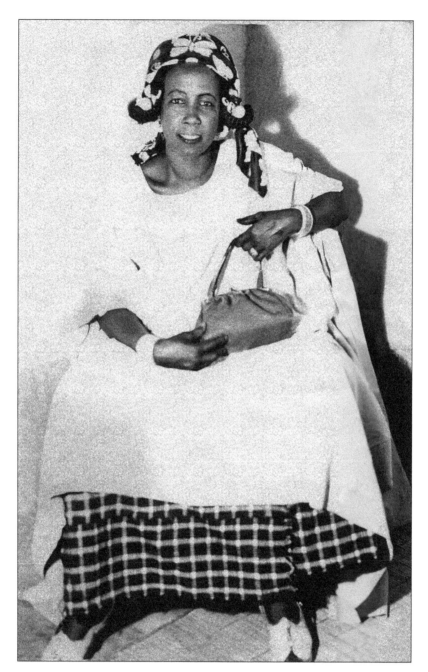

Grandmother Yaye Foune Mousso Sakiliba,
matriarch of the Thiam Clan

**Grandparents, Martial Boeuf and wife Marie-Jeanne, French
Customs Officer and educator with the professor**

Pascal and Dad on the Niger River

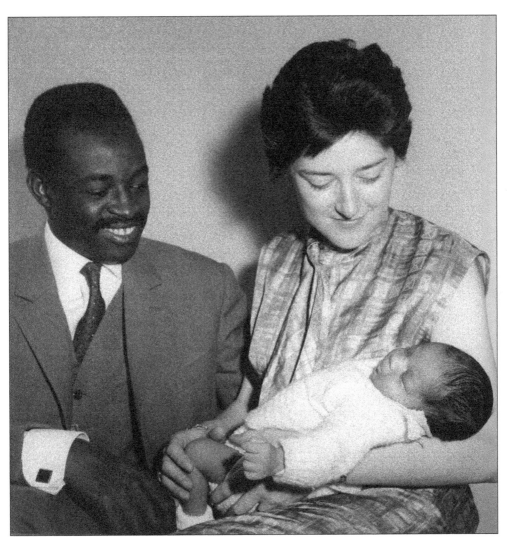

Abdou and Noelle Thiam, proud parents of the professor

Yaye with Pascal and sister Sarah

CONTENTS

INTRODUCTION

As a child of mixed Senegalese and French heritage who grew up in Mali, Senegal and France and whose journey led him to teach Jazz in the United States of America, I was always fascinated and intrigued by the level of cultural amnesia and the dearth of academic information that existed with respect to the socio-cultural contributions that West Africans taken from their continent through slavery had brought to the United States of America for 350 years.

As an outsider looking in, I was often puzzled by and sought to understand why European Americans generated dance moves and rhythmic expressions on the dance floors of the US that were closer in aesthetics to those of West Africans than the original dance moves of their informed European ethnic heritage from Vienna or the Paris Opera.

I struggled to figure out why the African American community clapped on beat two and four when expressing the rhythmic pulse of the music it created and how it was able to drive a whole nation whose majority was of European descent to integrate this sense of groove in its cultural norms, to the point where people would give you strange looks at a night club or a church if you were found clapping on the wrong beat, i.e. beat one.

It was particularly interesting to me since I know that in West Africa we clap on beat one and that Europeans also use beat one as their starting rhythmic referential point in the metric system of measures that codify their music.

In the absence of academic information, I tried to grasp why the vocal tonalities, inflexions, bent notes and rhythmic instrumental patterns of the rural Blues of the Mississippi Delta were so eerily reminiscent of the sounds of the ngoni, the songs of the Djalis and the melodic systems of the Soundiata Keita repertoire of eleventh century West Africa.

Lastly, I wanted to find out why the United States of America, a nation with an ethnic majority from Europe would incubate a music so vastly different from that of Baroque, Classical and Romantic European styles, that its identity markers laid in the bent and blue notes of its vocal stylings and instrumentations, the syncopation of its rhythms, the swing

feel of its expression and the harmonic and melodic tonalities of its oldest instrument of African descent, the banjo.

One of the issues confronting the assessment of the cultural relevance of West African contributions to North America and the world in general, was that the great majority of books or articles depicting such contributions had been written and published mostly by Europeans in academia, who although well-intended, were not issued from these sub Saharan African societies and thus lacked perspective and access to the knowledge, cultural foundation, subtleties, and sensibilities that only heritage in such traditions can inform soundly. Other European scholars writing about Africa and Africans for Africa, Africans and the world were simply blinded by their own prejudices and overtly promoted a sense of European cultural supremacy in line with the colonial thinking of the times. As early as the mid-nineteenth century, West Africa as a whole was mostly under French and British colonial rule from Senegal to Gambia, Guinea to Mali, Ivory Coast to Benin, Togo, to Tchad, Niger to Nigeria, Cameroon, etc. …

As expressed by African scholars Senghor, Cesaire, Diop, Leakey, Mazrui and echoed by British scholar Basil Davidson, it is of foremost importance that Africans define their heritage from the wealth of their languages and the horizon of their traditions. The purpose of this book is to look at the West African musical contributions and standards of aesthetics that have informed the music and the culture of the Mississippi Delta, in an effort to bridge this cultural and academic gap born out of a culture of indifference promulgated by former colonial institutions, out of respect for the unimaginable suffering, and in the memory of the millions of West Africans taken from their native lands for a period approximating three hundred and fifty years, and whose children paradoxically and intuitively created in the United States, drawing

from the depths of their collective souls the rhythmic, melodic and harmonic foundations of the musical traditions of the Mande, as expressed through the sonic landscape of the fieldhollers and worksongs, the Gospel and the Delta Blues, America's only indigenous artform Jazz.

Jazz in its aspirations and its blues, in its despair and its hopes embodies through creative rhythmic intuition the African forms of expression and the cultural standards of aesthetics of the African continent exacerbated by the poignantly violent and bloody socio-cultural experience of Africans and African Americans with American slavery, lynching, Jim Crow laws of segregation, economic, political and academic oppression in the United States.

The essence of Jazz steeped in the concepts of liberation, freedom and the highest cultural standards of aesthetics has ensured that Jazz will remain the symbolic art form of expression of oppressed people around the world. This journey began on the mighty banks of the Niger River. ...

West African Dancers at the White House

Young Americans dancing at the Disco

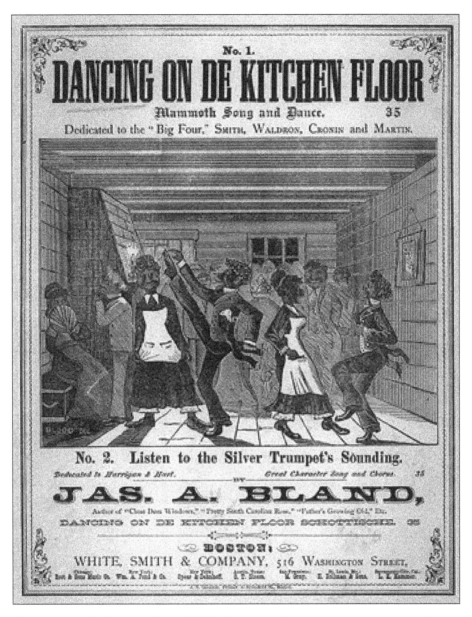

Dancing on de Kitchen Floor. 1880s sheet music cover, with cartoon carica-
tures of dancing African Americans. Song is by African American songwriter
James A. Bland.

CHAPTER 1

CULTURE OF WEST AFRICA

A.   HISTORICAL PERSPECTIVE

To better understand the significance of the cultural contributions of West Africans to North America we must first look to the chronology of the West African empires of that time. From the 5th century through the 17th century the Empires of Ghana, Mali and Songhai provide the background through which we come to appreciate the depth of the culture that exists in West Africa prior to the Atlantic Slave Trade. These African Empires are well organized, well administered and rely upon sophisticated taxation methods to stabilize and grow their respective economies. They have an extensive administrative structure that allows for the governance of large states of diverse population groups. These Empires create an architecture that defines their identities and their standards of aesthetics. Such architecture will later extend to the South of Spain in Andalucia and in the South of France past the Pyrennees.

The Empires of Ghana, Mali and Songhai manage an economy based on commerce, trade and agriculture. They have in place a military structure that supports them and secures their trading routes. As such, an artistic culture flourishes that involves the use of very specific musical instruments that can be found today in their present constitution, from which derives a musical repertoire of epic narratives and songs that is still sung today by the Djalis (musical and historian cast of West Africa).

From the 5th century until the 17th century, these three empires codify the cultural standards of aesthetics in education, in administration, in trade and commerce, in the arts, in medicine, in religion, in science and music. These standards of aesthetics had been defining the lives of these West African populations taken away from their native lands for centuries. The captured Africans will bring this civilizational background to the Americas from the 16th century through the 19th century. This intellectual and cultural life of West Africa is a known entity to European monarchies whose trade in gold and salt with the merchant dynasties of the city of Timbuktu is well documented (Caille, 1830).

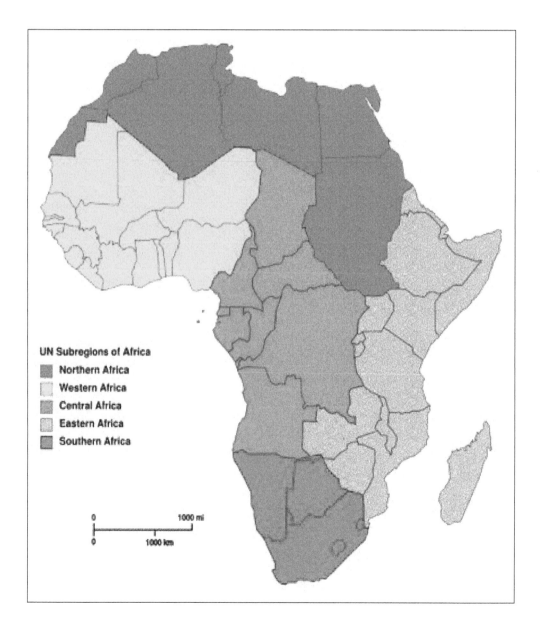

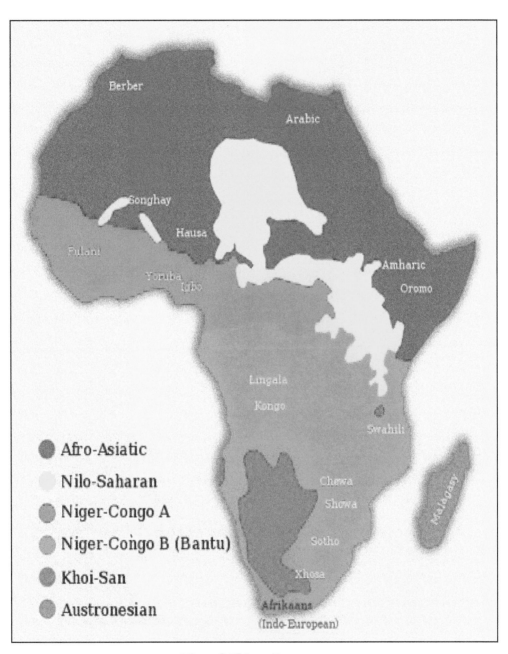

Map of African Languages

This map shows the consistency of cultural standards of aesthetics developed through a similarity of languages thus demonstrating the cultural sense of cohesion throughout West Africa and particularly with the states primarily afflicted with the Atlantic Slave Trade (red).

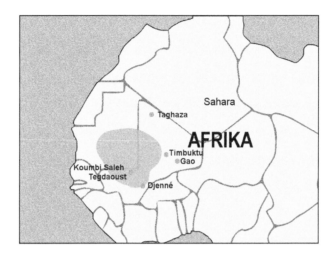

Ghana Empire, Capital Koumbi Saleh, 6th–11th century

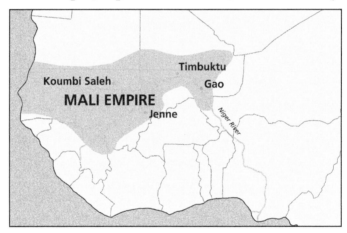

Mali Empire, Capital Timbuktu later Niani; 11th-14th century

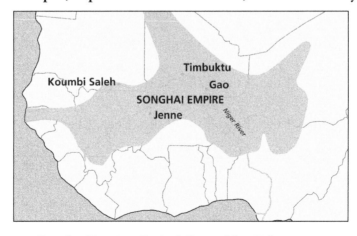

Songhai Empire, Capital Gao, 14th–17th century

Toumani Diabate, current torch holder of the Mande tradition

In 1325, Moroccan traveler Ibn Batouta writes of the existence of the West African instrument called ngoni (lute like) and the balafon (xylophone like) at the court of Malian Emperor Kankan Musa (Gibbs, 1929). The balafon is an important instrument in West Africa because of its fixed tonalities. These tonalities anchor the standards of aesthetics of harmony in West Africa and codify the melodies used in the Mande musical repertoire dedicated to the surnatural powers of Malian King Sunjata Keita. Sunjata Keita rules the empire of Mali during the 11th and 12th century. Today, the djalis continue to play the balafon, ngoni and kora in the performance of this Sunjata Keita repertoire that dates of the 12th century.

In academia, the kora or African harp is the instrument depicted by Scottish explorer Mungo Park in his travels to West Africa around 1799 (Park, 1799). The kora according to the Djalis of Mande is well over 1400 years old and certainly predates the balafon in the Mande (Diabate, 2008). Toumani Diabate, the current torch holder of the Mande historical tradition of the Sunjata Keita repertoire from the Diabate lineage of Djalis, indicates that he is the 71st generation of Diabate kora players. Thus, even by the most conservative accounts of mortality rates in West Africa, the kora would be in the range of 1450 to 1600 years old. The tuning of the kora would therefore infer that diatonic, major, minor and dominant tonality systems, including the use of blue notes exist in West Africa long before the five tone systems of the Gregorian chant modes present in Europe in the 7th and 8th century which themselves (Mazrui, 1988) derive from the Ethiopian Christian church repertoire.

Why do these epic narratives and body of songs of 11th and 12th century Sundiata Keita repertoire of West Africa matter? Simply because this body of songs and these instruments attest to the fact that high standards of aesthetics governing the role of the voice, governing harmony (major third, minor third at the octave creating the sharp nine concept), melody, counterpoint (both hands on the kora creating simultaneous counterpuntal melodic systems), rhythm (steadiness of tempos and pulses), polyrhythm (superimposition of rhythmic figures resolving sequentially), phrasing, musical expression and improvisation using pentatonic, diatonic, heptatonic, blue notes, the use of the dominant seven tone in a major seven tone system which appropriate implementation during improvisation is central to the aesthetics of Malian sensibilities, and the microtonic harmonic and melodic systems are already in place in 11th and 12th century West Africa.

Lastly, we know that during the Atlantic slave trade balafon players were brought to North America. The Virginia Gazette of 1776 records Africans playing a "barafoo" an instrument which looks like a balafon (Southern, 1976).

A young balafon player, Mali

**Jeweler Gallo Thiam
and the Kora Players**

The presence of these three Empires Ghana, Mali and Songhai indicate that from the 5th through the 18th century there are in West Africa, all along the banks of the Niger River, communities of Africans who have generated conceptual frameworks of intellectual references defining excellence in the arts, architecture, sciences, religious discipline, education, administration that indicate a high degree of civilization. That high level of community standards, socio-cultural and intellectual references which we find all along the Niger River consequently binds the people who will later be taken as slaves to the New World and for our purpose more specifically to the plantations of North America. West African standards of aesthetics are felt more acutely in the emerging culture of the South of the United States because it is primarily the place where we encounter the greatest concentration of West Africans brought during the Atlantic slave trade, thus generating a rural musical style which will later be termed "Blues".

Basekou Kouyate performing on a Ngoni

Papa Diabate performing on a Kora

Taj Mahal performing on a banjo

Honeyboy Edwards performing on a blues guitar

Mandinka woman with gold earrings symbolizing social status

These West African standards of aesthetics will provide the foundation for this emerging music and the expression of socio-cultural traits that defines the life and identity of the African and African American community in the geographical area referred to as the Delta. These standards of aesthetics will manifest themselves through the rhythmic, melodic, and harmonic patterns of the fieldhollers, the worksongs, the voodoo rituals and the final harmonic, rhythmic and melodic conceptualization of the Delta Blues. They explain why the foundation of American popular music born out of the Mississippi Delta Blues created by the African social experience in North America through slavery has more to do with West African cultural standards of aesthetics than the musical standards of Vienna or the Paris Opera of those days.

Mandinka dancing

Sosso djembe & balafon

B: **NIGER RIVER: WEST AFRICAN CULTURAL HIGHWAY OF CENTRAL SIGNIFICANCE**

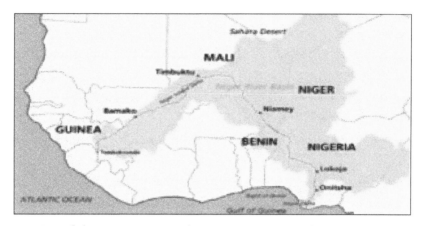

Map of the Niger River and Niger River Basin, shown in green

To appreciate how cultural standards of aesthetics travelled and permeated the various ethnic groups of West Africa, we need to look at the paramount cross-cultural fertilization role the Niger River played, economically, socially and linguistically in the dissemination of such information. Sourcing in the southeastern part of Guinea, approximately 240 miles inland from the Atlantic ocean the Niger River takes an unusual route as it heads away from the sea toward the Sahara Desert to the important imperial cultural cities of Timbuktu, Djenne, Gao, Segou and Mopti before coming back south to the Gulf of Guinea and the Delta of Nigeria.

Boats on the Niger River unloading blocks of salt from Taoudeni being just like it was done ancestrally

During the respective eras of the Empires of Ghana, Mali and Songhai, this river served as the development point of these West African civilizations. The Niger River supplied life and trade through navigation and commerce. Socio-cultural exchanges took place with the various ethnic societies that bordered the banks of the river. The Niger provided a lifeline to the semi-arid western Sahelian zone. It was a way of life for many of the ethnic groups (Mandinkas, Maninkas, Malinkes, Songhai, Sossos etc. …) who will codify the societal norms and values in West Africa. The Niger River supplied livelihood to the Bozos who were fishermen, irrigation to the Bambaras or Malinkes who were farmers, and transportation to the herders of Touareg and Fula descent.

The Niger River is approximately 2,600 miles and it links the countries of Guinea, Mali, Niger, Nigeria, Benin, Burkina Faso, Cameroon, Chad, and Ivory Coast. Most of these countries were at one point or another part of, or under the Empires of Ghana, Mali and/or Songhai socio-cultural rule and administrative influence. The Atlantic Slave Trade centered on such countries.

The civilizational depths of these three empires coupled with the centuries of cross-cultural fertilization on the banks of the Niger River explain the common cultural identity traits found in the various ethnic groups of West Africa. These cultural traits are born out of the convictions of polytheism, the necessity of the oral tradition as the preferred mode of transference of knowledge, the subdivision of polyrhythmic syncopated patterns, the constant rhythmic interplay of three against two generating this sense of balance or pulse which will later be termed "swing", and a philosophy of life that while differing on the margins depending on the geographic location of these ethnic groups remains strongly anchored in a uniquely West African sense of community linking religious and secular life rituals, with an identity of philosophical and intellectual historical perspectives.

Crossing of the Niger River

These traits are exemplified through the study of epic narratives, the etymology, the linguistic concepts and the articulation of grammatical rules, the philosophical appreciation of symbolism where expression is not necessarily a function of what is but rather a function of what it suggests, the social codification of family names, and the notions of social status through the organization of the caste system. These common cultural identity traits are expressed culturally in ceremonies and musically through the celebration of the Sunjata Keita musical repertoire. The use of the koras, balafons, ngonis, and djembes and all their related string and percussion offsprings throughout West Africa, coupled with a reliance on the standards of aesthetics that define rhythm, harmony and melody bind these diverse population groups so to infuse them with an unmistakable sense of identity which is expressed through this appreciation for and of rhythm which colors the landscape of all socio-cultural life in West Africa.

The West African cultural citadels of Koumbi Saleh, Timbuktu, Gao, Djenne, Mopti, Niani, Segou, Niamey, Lokoja and Onitsha all of which border the banks of the Niger River, as shown on the map below, alternate as beacons of influence between the 6th and 17th century. Between the 5th and 17th century, the Niger River is the economic and cultural unifying engine of West Africa. While the cities through their architecture provide testimony to the significance of their cultural historical legacy and the role they played in the shaping of the socio-economics of these West African kingdoms, these cities were cultural and administrative institutions which boasted the best trade centers with great open markets where business was conducted by populations from various ethnic groups from, Sub-Saharan Africa, North Africa, East Africa, Europe, as well as populations from the Arabic Peninsula.

Passengers travelling on the banks of the Niger River at Gao

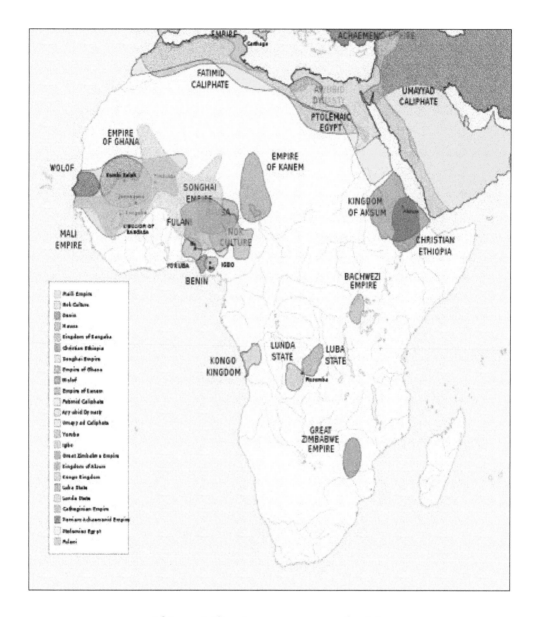

African civilizations map—pre-colonial

CHAPTER 2

MEDIEVAL WEST AFRICAN EMPIRES

Three Empires Ruling West Africa from the 6th Century through the 16th

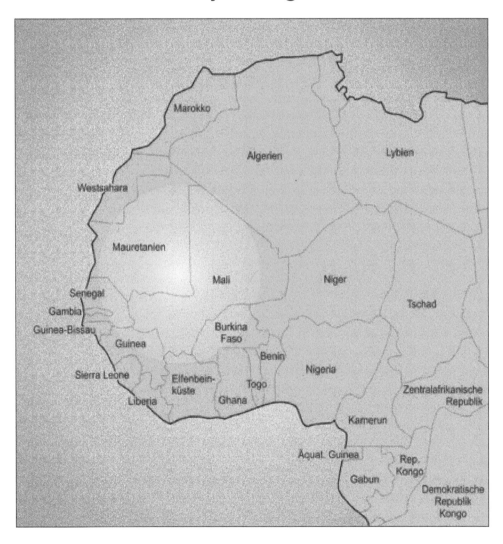

Empire of Ghana and its cultural influence during medieval period

A: THE EMPIRE OF GHANA

Established by the Soninkes sub-Saharan Africans between 650 and 1076 the Empire of Ghana or Wagadou Empire (land of the herds) extends from the south of Mauritania, to the western part of Mali, and the eastern part of Senegal. Sanhaja traders or Berber nomads tell stories about the kingdom in the eighth century which are later corroborated by the scholar from Cordoba, Al-Bakri who gave detailed descriptions of the customs and rituals of the inhabitants of the empire (Bakri, 1068).

The Empire of Ghana (Ghana is also title of the emperor) is the first of the three Empires (Ghana, Mali and Songhai) that defined a sub-saharan civilization through its administration, its governmental reach, its trading practices and commerce, its cultural influence through the arts, and the application of its military strength. The extensive trade of gold, ivory and salt coupled with the introduction of the camel as a mode of transportation for manufactured goods led to an acceleration of the regional commerce and trade routes linking the sub-saharan regions to North Africa, Europe and the Middle East. Large urban centers grow and expanded territories allowed for additional trading routes. A complex system of taxation permitted the empire to expand administratively and strengthen its armies. Ghana at its apogee had an army exceeding 200,000 men patrolling its trade routes.

During Soninke rule the religious practices were mostly a combination of West African rituals and animists ceremonies. Islamic practices although tolerated by Soninke rulers were not embraced by the population at large, however, Soninke rulers enforced tolerance and freedom of religion and Muslims were allowed their choice of faith and worship practices. In keeping with polytheistic traditions, legend has it that the early religion of the kingdom involved the worship of the Emperor of Ghana but also that of a mythical water serpent Bida'a who ruled the Niger River. During the empire of Ghana's administration the capital is Kombi Saleh and the languages spoken are Soninkes and Malinkes.

Internal strife diminished the Empire of Ghana. The Soninkes engaged in a succession of military battles with the Sosso people led by Diarra Kante. His son Soumaoro Kante will end the era of the Empire of Ghana. The victorious Sossos will annex the goldmines of Bure in state of Kangaba. The Sossos who do not accept Islam and its practices advocate a return to African ancestral traditions and religious beliefs. Around 1230, the Mande people of the state of Kangaba led by a young prince by the name of Sunjata Keita will rebel against Sosso rule and defeat Soumaoro Kante at the battle of Kirina in 1235. This battle announces the rise of the people of Mande who will define an era, and a civilization known as the Empire of Mali.

Rulers of the Empire of Ghana, Soninke ethnic group of West Africa

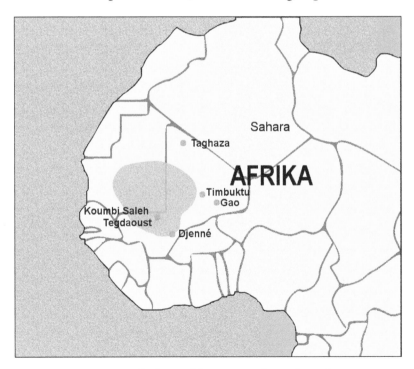

Empire of Ghana 6th century through 12th
Capital Koumbu Saleh
Ethnic rulers Soninkes

Elderly Soninke Man

Sarrakholes, Soninkes Warriors (illustration de *Côte occidentale d'Afrique*, 1890 du Colonel Frey

Soninke woman and little girl

B.   THE EMPIRE OF MALI

The rise of the Mande or Mandinka people led by their first king Sunjata Keita heralds a new era in West Africa. The Empire of Mali and its civilization begins in 1230 through 1600. Founded by Sunjata Keita (a ruler of mythical proportion), the culture of Mali has deep and far reaching influences in West Africa. This empire which at its apex is composed of many states managed by vassal kings who have pledged allegiance to the emperor covers a surface area larger than Western Europe. The rulers of Mali have been depicted by medieval scholars in superlative terms and the name of the City of Timbuktu has remained forever attached in history to the metaphors of opulence, gold, academic and religious universities, bustling trade and prosperous commerce.

The title of the emperor of Mali is Mansa and the capital of the Malian empire was Niani. A complex administrative process organized the empire of Mali. It involved a combination of allied states and conquered regions which were given administrative and economic autonomy as long as they pledged allegiance to the Mansa and its descendants. A deliberative body the "Kouroukan Fouga," the equivalent of a modern form of a national assembly or "Gbara" with regional representation and clan delegations, was put in place to manage the administrative and economic affairs of the empire. Reforms were put in place to address and prohibit the mistreatment of slaves and prisoners, to install women in position of influence and to organize a system of fixed exchange rates for common goods that were fair to all provinces.

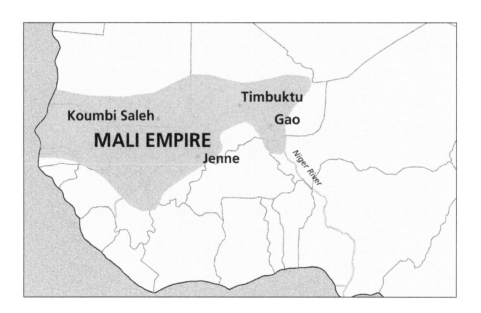

Extent of the Mali Empire 12th through 15th century.
Capital Timbuktu & Niani

After Sunjata Keita, we will count an excess of twenty Mansas to rule the empire. The lineage and the accomplishments of these rulers are passed on through the oral tradition of the Djalis (musical and historian cast). These Mansas extended the borders of the Empire of Mali beyond imagination and ruled over most of West Africa, annexing the lands of the Bambaras, Peuhls, Woloffs, Serers, Songhai and Tuaregs. At one point the empire ruled over 400 cities. The most famous of Mansas was Kankan Musa. History remembers him fondly for his generosity and his epic pilgrimage to Mecca. He is said to have given so much gold during his journey to Mecca that it took twelve years for the price of gold to regain its currency in Cairo, Egypt. The Mansa Musa built Timbuktu into a modern academic city, with high standards of aesthetics of architecture, science, administrative and religious studies, arts and commerce.

The engine of the economy of the Malian Empire was trade in gold, salt and an efficient system of taxation. A steady tax revenue base and the help of a powerful and organized military structure allowed the empire of Mali to expand its land acquisition process. The gold mines of Bambuk, Boure and Galam provided the empire with unsurpassed wealth and comfort (Stride, 1971). By the 14th century, the Empire of Mali provided half of the world's export of gold. The Empire of Mali was known for the stability of its governmental institutions and its disciplined transition of power. According to a 1929 English translation, the scholar Ibn Battuta who visited the area in 1352 AD said this about its inhabitants;

> *"The negroes possess some admirable qualities.*
> *They are seldom unjust, and have a greater abhorrence of injustice than any other*
> *people. There is complete security in their country. Neither traveler nor inhabitant in*
> *it has anything to fear from robbers or men of violence."*
>
> (Gibb, 1929).

While there is academic controversy around the epics of the Malian Empire none have generated the level of stridence as the Malian expedition of Mansa Abubakri II in 1311. He is said to have had an interest in the western sea and joined thousands of vessels equipped with oars and sails to the conquest of the Atlantic (Person, 1968). While neither the Mansa nor anyone else made it back to the empire, the records of this account are preserved in North Africa and in the oral tradition of the Djalis of Mali. However, evidence of Mande writings and artifacts were found in Central America at the anthropological location of the Olmecs (Wiener, 1922).

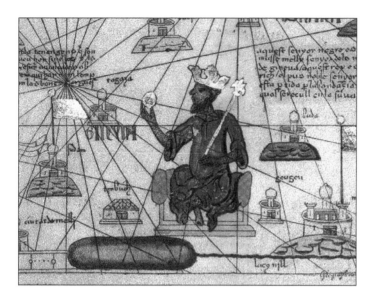

Mansa Musa depicted holding a gold nugget from a 1395 map of Africa and Europe

Eventually, abuses of power and mismanagement of the empire coupled with battles with an emerging Songhai uprising, Touareg revolts, Bamana rebellions, and Moroccan infiltrations led to the decline and fall of the Empire of Mali in 1667.

Market day at Banamba, Mali

Young woman from Mali

Cattle herder man from Mali

C.   THE EMPIRE OF SONGHAI

A small Songhai state had existed since the 11th century and had been subjected to the rules of the Empires of Ghana and Mali successively. Its political and economical base was located on the northeastern part of the Niger River. The Songhai Empire will be one of the largest African Empires. The capital of the Songhai Empire was Gao. Its most illustrious emperor was Sonni Ali. Steeped in the teachings of Islam and reigning from about 1464 to 1493 Ali, a first rate military commander, annexed many of the Songhai's neighboring states, including what remained of the Malian Empire. He regained control of the critical trade routes and wrestled cities such as Timbuktu, and Djenne from Touareg dominance. Sonni Ali brought immense wealth to the Songhai Empire. He is remembered as an emperor who did not impose Islam to non Muslim populations and is acknowledged for stressing the importance and the need for his subjects to rely on African religions, philosophies and traditions.

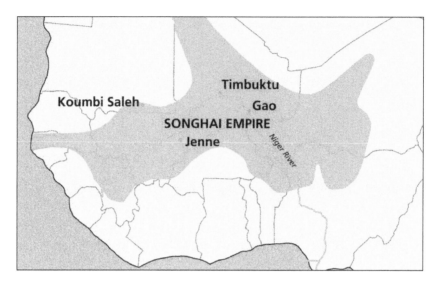

**The Songhai Empire, from 15th to 17th century,
Capital: Gao**

One of the reasons for the economic success of the Songhai Empire had to do with the precision of its administrative and military structures. Trade was safe throughout the empire for it had standing armies stationed in each province ready to intervene at any given time. Merchants were protected and port cities on the banks of the Niger River guarded. Gold, salt and slaves remained the major staples of this trans-Saharan trade. An intricate system of taxation and the organization of courts of justice allowed for a civil society to develop and prosper. Administrative decentralization of power and reliance on local and state ethnic governmental structures were also important factors in the stability, success and longevity of the Songhai Empire. In 1550 troubles in the succession of power occurred, signaling the decline of the Songhai Empire. The sultan of Morocco Ahmad Al Mansur and his forces armed with gunpowder weapons routed the Songhai armies at Gao, Timbuktu and Djenne in 1591, effectively ending Songhai hegemony.

Songhai pottery at market

D.   CIVILIZATIONAL DIMENSION AND CULTURAL SIGNIFICANCE

Several books would be needed to thoroughly inform the reader about the depth and cultural reach of these three empires, Ghana, Mali and Songhai, empires which commanded and organized so much of the socio-cultural life of West Africa and beyond. The cultural and civilizational importance of these three empires lays in their longevity, the stability they demonstrated and the degrees of complexities involved in the economic, administrative, and military management of these vast and diverse territories populated by ethnically diverse communities.

The fact that these empires ruled West Africa and played an important role as equal trading partners to European kingdoms for the better part of twelve consecutive centuries is testimony to the success and the administrative, economic, social balance and military abilities of its ruling classes. While slavery was a part of the social fabric of these respective empires, the debasement of an individual with the status of slave was never accepted or condoned in West Africa.

Servitude was an integral part of the social life of West Africa. West African kingdoms routinely enrolled in bondage prisoners of wars as well as individuals foreign or national who needed to pay a debt to society for violating societal norms and values. We should note that culturally West Africans never believed that the concept of prison was an effective method of social redress and as a result we will not see an incarceration system in place in West Africa until the arrival of Europeans. The idea of locking men up, feeding them while they sat on their hands not useful to the communities they abused was foreign to these West African populations. Instead, these West African communities put convicted felons to work through an elaborate system of indentured servitude which often lasted a lifetime and whose status was not passed on to their children. The justice system was in accordance to rules and regulations in effect in these territories. In many cases some modified versions of Islamic law was applied. Justice was served swiftly by the King or the Quadis (religious leaders). In his 14th century memoirs of travels, Ibn Batouta had this to say about West Africans in Mali;

> *"My stay at Niani lasted about fifty days, and I was shown honor and entertainment by its inhabitants … they are seldom unjust, and have a greater abhorrence of injustice than any other people.*
>
> *Their sultan shows no mercy to anyone who is guilty of the least act of it. There is complete security in their country. Neither traveler nor inhabitant in it has anything to fear from robbers or men of violence the blacks do not confiscate the goods of any North Africans who may die in their country, not even when these consist of large treasures. On the contrary they deposit these goods with a man of confidence until those who have a right to the goods present themselves and take possession."*
> Ibn Batouta, 14th century (Gibb, 1958)

In the absence of a prison system, prisoners of war became the property of the wealthy families of the state who won the wars. These prisoners began to serve their new victors within these territorial jurisdictions. These slaves were protected as a symbol of wealth but also integrated within the local family structures. As a result of this philosophy of lifestyle, slaves and slavemasters coexisted and developed socio-cultural bonds that allowed for slaves to rise from their subjugated status to that of adviser and sometimes even administrative leaders of the communities that enslaved them.

The existence of these West African Empires demonstrates the acute level of civilization and administrative might in place to manage the urban centers and the vast territories populated by such diverse populations. It further shows the academic know how these empires exemplified in their day to day management of this enormous wealth that resulted in the long-lasting powers they exercised for centuries from the Atlantic to the Mediterranean basin and beyond. Their existence also reflects the determination of its monarchs and its ruling classes to extend always further the borders of their nations, their ability to manage and secure in-land trade routes and/or water ways, through the establishment of a sophisticated military machine (sometimes exceeding 200,000 infantry men and 50,000 cavalry as well as a significant naval presence to ensure the safety of the waterways of the Niger River) and a highly developed taxation system.

The level of importance of these empires as generators of wealth and comfort through trade to the rest of Europe is demonstrated by the academic and economic influence and level of affluence of its urban centers. Timbuktu, Djenne, Niani, Segou, Mopti and Gao are a testimony to the diplomatic and socio-economic relationships these empires had with other African and non-African peoples. The cultural unity of Sub-Saharan Africa through its empires is well documented, analyzed and verified by eminent scholars such as Cheikh Anta Diop (Diop, 1959) and Basil Davidson (Davidson, 1984).

Relying heavily on cavalry but incorporating infantry as well, the empires of Ghana, Mali, and Songhai dominated large parts of West Africa for centuries.

Fourri; King of Accra, Ghana, 18th century

During the eras of the empires of Ghana, Mali and Songhai war-canoes were constructed of a single log, with inner space for rowers and warriors, and facilities such as hearths and sleeping quarters. Some measured up to 80 feet and could accommodate 100 soldiers. Warriors and rowers were armed with bow, shield and spear. Firearms increasingly supplemented traditional weapons.

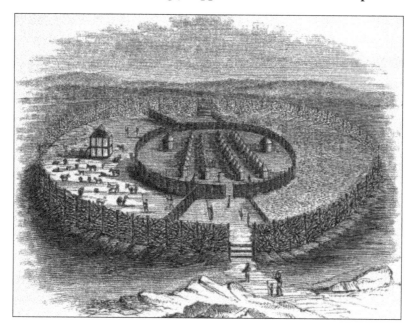

Fortifications were important in African warfare and societies. The ramparts of 15th century Benin are described as the world's most extensive earthwork according to the Guinness Book of Records.

Duala war-canoe, Cameroon, 19th century

Left: Fourri; King of Accra, Ghana, 18th century. *Right:* Kwaku Dua III Asamu or Nana Akwasi Agyeman Prempeh I (1872-1931), king (Asentehene) of the Ashanti Confederacy in West Africa.

CHAPTER 3

TRADE ROUTES TO EUROPE, THE ARABIC PENINSULA AND ASIA

A. TRADE ROUTES

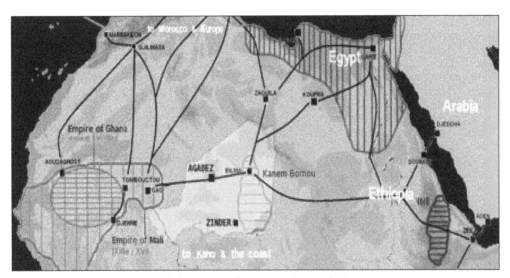

Saharan trade routes circa 1400

The Saharan trade routes created a mosaic of urban commerce centers that extended from the Sub-Saharan West African empires of Ghana, Mali and Songhai and connected West Africa across the Sahara desert to Europe, the Arabic Peninsula through the Red Sea, the Eastern seaboard or Swahili coast to Asia. For a period approximating thirteen centuries the trade of gold, salt, slaves, food items, crafts, leather goods, cotton cloth, and metal ornaments links the West African Empires of Ghana, Mali and Songhai to the European Kingdoms of the Franks with Clovis, and Charlemagne, through Phillip le Bel and the Knight Templars through Louis the XIVth.

These trade routes are important because they allowed for the dissemination of African cultural musical standards of aesthetics through the travels of African itinerant musicians. European medieval literature refer to them as troubadours playing the luth, except that this "luth" is really the African ould or sintir which is one of the most common musical instrument from regional Mali extending to North Africa.

At the height of the effervescence of the Sub-Saharan African trade routes to Europe and Asia, Koumbi Saleh was the economic capital of the Empire of Ghana, as was Timbuktu to the Empire of Mali and Jenne and Gao to the Empire of Songhai.

Modern-day camel caravan near the Ahaggar Mountains
in the central Sahara

B.   THE EMPIRE OF GHANA TRADE ROUTES AND THE NIGER RIVER

Rich in gold, the Empire of Ghana was located in a large land area that extended to today's Senegal, Mali, Mauritania, Niger, and Guinea. Gold and salt were the main commodities of trade and salt sold for almost as much of gold. Salt found in the desert regions of Morocco and Algeria was traded by Arab merchants via caravans of camels travelling from the Mediterranean basin into the heart of West African kingdoms.

From the village of Sidjilmassa in Morocco through the Sahara desert the trading routes linked the village of Taghaza known for its high quality salt to the gold region of the Empire of Ghana located near the Senegal River of the Bambuk and Bure states.

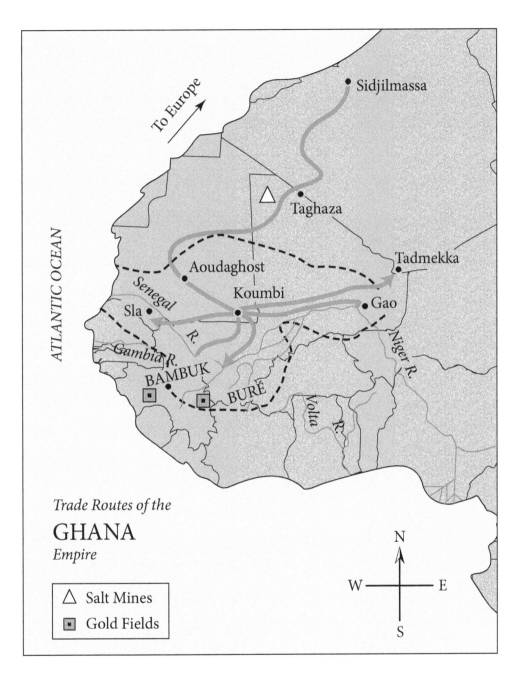

Gold, Salt Trade Map of Empire of Ghana

C. SAHARAN TRADE DURING THE EMPIRE OF MALI

The rise of the Empire of Mali in 1235 led to the fall of the Empire of Ghana. Despite political upheavals, Mali maintained control of the gold-salt trade routes and expanded trading posts all the way to Tunisia and Egypt. Tunis and Cairo to the North would become important trading centers that connected to Timbuktu and Djenne to the south strengthening the economic lifeline of West Africa.

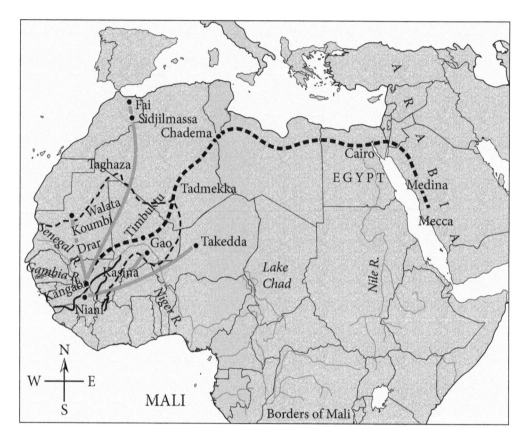

Trade Map of Empire of Mali

These new trade routes from the Empire of Mali to Tunisia and Egypt ushered what will become a long tradition of statesmen's visits between the northern territories of Tunis and Cairo and the West African Empires of Sub-Saharan Africa. One of the most famous visits to Cairo and Mecca is that of Malian Emperor Mansa Musa in1324. The Mansa's generosity became legendary and his journey to Mecca remains in the archives of medieval Africa and Egypt for its splendor and opulence. He traveled with thousands of subjects that included musicians who would sing his praises and chronicled this phenomenal journey.

D.   THE SONGHAY EMPIRE AND TRANS-SAHARAN TRADE

Sonni Ali Kolon led the Songhay people to challenge the Malian empire in the late 1400s. The control of the trade centers of Timbuktu and Jenne on the banks of the Niger River were centrally important to the Songhai in the administrative, economic and military management of the trade routes of the empire. The city of Gao which had developed under the Malian empire and had grown in population and economic relevance will see its zenith during Sonni Ali's reign.

Salt caravan from Agadez to Bilma, 1985

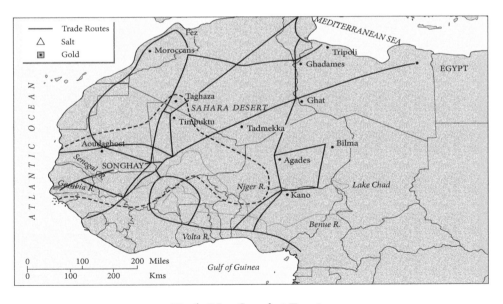

Trade Map Songhai Empire

CHAPTER 4

✵

WEST AFRICAN CIVILIZATIONAL CENTERS

Timbuktu and its patrons

To assess the high degree of civilizational concepts present in West Africa between the 5th and 17th centuries one only has to look at the history of the great urban centers of Koumbi Saleh, Timbuktu, Djenne, Gao, Mopti, and Segou. These centers exemplify excellence in administration and in the management of complex trade routes covering vast land areas, in the dispensation of academic and religious knowledge, in the support of the arts and in the development of cultural standards of aesthetics that these West African populations who travel to the Americas and North America will conceptually bring with them through the 350 years of the Atlantic Slave Trade.

A local resident of Tombouctou, Mali, looks out of his window

Aguibou, Fama of Bandiagara, son of El-Hadj-Omar.
Very old and powerful family of Macina

A.   THE GREAT CITY OF KOUMBI SALEH

Koumbi Saleh, capital of the Empire of Ghana of the West African Soninke people, was located south of the current Mauritania. It served as the administrative tax and trade center of salt, gold, spices and humans for the caravans en route for North Africa, the Arabic Peninsula, Europe and Asia. At its apogee the population of Koumbi Saleh exceeded 30,000 citizens. The archeological sites were rediscovered in 1913.

According to historian El Bakri in 1067, the Emperor of Ghana whose seat was at Koumbi Saleh and was animist allowed for Muslims to live, prosper and worship in that great city. It is one of the early testimonies in West Africa in which socio-economic development takes place with the cultural acceptance of multi faiths social worships. The Emperor held court covered in gold surrounded by princes, vassals, judges and soldiers and adjudicated matters of the State and citizens' disputes. The Emperor of Ghana could raise at any time an army in excess of 200,000 men to address conflicts, patrol trade routes and enforce his rule.

B.   THE GREAT CITY OF TIMBUKTU

Timbuktu, for the better part of 800 years, was a towering civilizational center in West Africa for trade and commerce, education and religion, science and architecture. Its citizens administered and managed some of the most important trading routes for the commerce

of gold, salt, slaves and crafts across the Sahara to Morocco, Algeria and Europe through the Mediterranean basin, Egypt and Asia. Timbuktu set standards all over the world for the organization of its military structures that allowed for the management of its trading routes in great safety.

The precision and the administration of its trading practices, its banking and taxation methods, the depth of its academic studies in the arts, sciences and religion made it a cultural beacon all over the world in medieval times. Located on the edge of the Sahara Desert, and on the banks of the Niger River, Timbuktu's elegant and high architecture reflected the rich heritage of a powerful economic trading and intellectual center informed by deep West African traditions, standards of aesthetics, Islamic influences and the secularization of its evolving times through its trade practices with the Mediterranean Basin.

Mosques, which are Islamic religious centers for worship, were erected in Timbuktu in the form of monumental buildings for the times. These religious centers for worship also served as universities of great scholarship where men of letters from all over the world would congregate and write. These mosques such as the Sankore Mosque housed universi-

Sankore Mosque of Timbuktu, Mali

ties and libraries where rare and precious manuscripts were kept. In Timbuktu, affluent families from the various cast structures decorated the doors of their villas in ornamented fashions that expressed both their social standing and their wealth. Timbuktu became a place where one could acquire an education, in the arts, sciences or religion, as well as wealth and social status. The splendor of the University of Timbuktu was unrivaled in Africa and radiated throughout the pan-Islamic world and beyond.

The books and manuscripts that were written at the height of Timbuktu's civilizational radiance around the 14th century in the areas of science and religion, poetry and mathematics can still be found today in the custody of certain families of this great city.

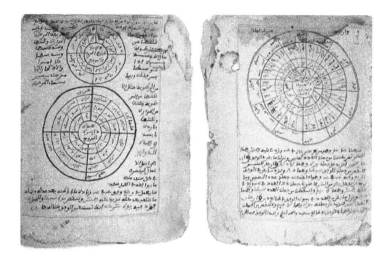

Timbuktu Manuscripts

These manuscripts, whose wealth of information still awes contemporary scholars, are testimony to the high level of civilization that existed in West Africa in medieval times and to the scholarship of its inhabitants who will later be subjected to the Atlantic slave trade.

Ancient manuscripts maintained at Timbuktu's Ahmed Baba Center and in private family libraries, such as the Mamma Haidara Commemorative Library and the Library of Cheick Zayni Baye of Boujbeha, a suburb of Timbuktu, remind us of the academic brilliance of Timbuktu and its influence beginning in the 15th and 16th centuries.

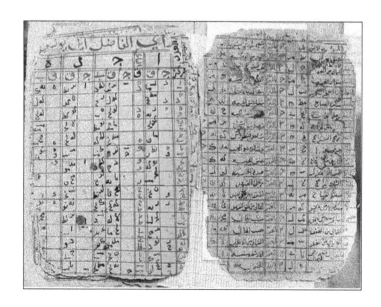

Timbuktu Cloth Sellers

C.   THE GREAT CITY OF DJENNÉ

Founded around 250 B.C.E. by the Bozo people at a site named Djenné-Jeno, Djenné is situated in south-central Mali. Djenne was an important trading center in the trans-Saharan trade of gold, salt and slaves. With its conversion to Islam in the 11th century, Djenne rivaled Timbuktu in affluence. Its academic centers for religious studies and academic excellence in the arts and sciences became famous all over the medieval world and wealthy merchants from the Mediterranean basin began to make Djenne their residence of choice. The great mosque of Djenne and its academic institutes who hosted thousands of students was a treasured beacon of West African architectural prowess in masonry during the middle Ages. Evidence of this monumental mosque is still present today.

Market at Djenne, Mali

D.   THE GREAT CITY OF GAO

Conquered by the Malian Empire before the 14th century, Gao was founded around the 7th century and later became the capital of the Songhai Empire. Gao quickly rose as a center of trade and learning, culturally connected with the great Trans-Saharan trade cities of Timbuktu and Djenne. An important industrial city, it had a very strong manufacturing base that provided labor to a large urban population (Tim Insoll, 1997).

Under the leadership of Songhai Emperor (Askia) Sonni Ali Ber, Gao boasted a 1,000-boat navy on the Niger River, a large military structure with organized cavalry regiments, a flourishing mercantile base, and an academic life whose brilliance rivaled that of Djenne and Timbuktu.

View of the pink dunes from the tomb of the Askia Mohamed

The city of Gao was a model of administrative efficiency with complex and effective taxation methods, standardized weights and measure systems, an impressive justice system and a set of advisory boards that enabled the governor to deftly manage the affairs of this large urban center.

In Gao, at the tomb of its leader the Askia Mohamed

E.   THE GREAT CITY OF SEGOU AND ITS KINGDOM

A power vacuum created by the Moroccan invasion of 1591 signaled the end of the Songhai Empire. The instability generated by this invasion of the large land areas formerly controlled by the Songhai produced a political vacuum that will be filled by an ascending regional power located along the banks of the Niger River, the Bamana or Bambara people.

The City of Ségou-Koro became the administrative and political center of this emerging power. The platform for military expansion and political rule of the Bamana people of West Africa was born out of the indigenous social structures that fostered a sense of communal responsibility and social equality based on the caste system, away from Islamic precepts.

The intellectual and religious order of Bamana societies were articulated around the importance of understanding the mystical spheres of knowledge that evade Cartesian understanding, and the need to communicate with the paranormal through the making of metaphysically potent substances, to channel vast resources of supernatural energy for socio-cultural and spiritual purposes. The traditional social order in Bamana societies was organized around the notion of age and merit. As such, these societies were governed by a council of elders. Younger men operated in trade guilds, and formed associations based on principles of mutual cooperation and shared resources.

Ségou-Koro grew in importance during the 17th century under the reign of the Coulibalys and King Mamary Coulibaly also named Biton will establish his authority and a lasting legacy for the whole region. Biton joined the great trading centers of Timbuktu, Macina and Jenne to the kingdom of Segou. Under Biton's reign, architecture, craftsmanship and the musical arts flourished (Bortholot, 2000).

Ahmadou, roi de Ségou Ahmadu Tall (var. Ahmadu Seku/Sekou) Toucouleur ruler (Almami) of Ségou (now Mali) from 1864–1892

The Bambaras or Bamana societies are people from the land of Mande. This is important because it indicates that during the kingdom of Segou in the 17th century while the Atlantic slave trade rages there is a consciousness of the value of the arts in West Africa. With King Biton, there is a resurgence of the musical repertoire of Mande or Soundiata Keita repertoire with the power of the cast of Djalis becoming more prominent. This rise of interests in the shoring up of the musical arts under Biton signals the continuity and the depth of the civilizational influence that generated the musical melodic, harmonic and rhythmic standards of aesthetics that Africans taken as slaves from these regions will bring to North America to inform what will be termed later "Blues".

Colorful crowd at the market in Mali

CHAPTER 5

AFRICAN CULTURAL CONCEPTS
EXPRESSED THROUGH THE ARTS

A. RHYTHMIC INTUITION

To appreciate the music, the culture and the innate sense of rhythm that permeates all of African American forms of expression in the African American community, scholars Leopold Sedar Senghor, Aime Cesaire and Henri Bergson, through their theoretical concepts of identity linked to the notions of rhythmic intuition and creative intelligence, give us a window on the socio-cultural mechanism of societal transfers of cultural standards of aesthetics through the arts.

Given the intuitive and objective notions of cultural references shared by a commonality of aesthetic traits and sensibilities due to a geographical proximity and an historical relational ancestrality, it is understandable that, as a result of the depth of the shared socio-cultural trauma represented in the experience of slavery in North America, these West African populations' brought in bondage for more than three centuries will dig to the deepest of their intuitive collective soul to pull out and project onto any medium of expression that which is so important to their inner, mental, psychological, emotional and intimate identity as a mechanism of survival. That which is pulled out of the depth of these West African populations collective cultural soul is that which is so essential to their sense of identity borne out of this intuitive sense of creativity moved by an innate energy flow that we call RHYTHM but more importantly it is a concept that West Africans define as STEADY MOTION FLOW or what we refer to in America as GROOVE.

STEADY expresses the appreciation of the space that exists between two beats or entities. MOTION expresses the nature of the feeling of pulse generated by the rhythmic opposition of three against two, six against eight, twelve against eight that Africans create in their relational rhythmic expression of sound wave vibrations. America's foremost composer Edward Kennedy Ellington will name this phenomenon "Swing". FLOW expresses the creative intuitive energy that moves all animated beings transferred into action.

It is important to note that such an expression of rhythm is a conceptual notion of energy flow that extends not only to musical expression through musical instruments but also to the choice of colors, the illustration of themes in paintings, the lines in fashion, the cut in the clay, the verse in the song, the rhyme in poetry, and to the rhythmic verbal delivery of the text that transferred from West Africa to the South of the United States as demonstrated in the oration of the African Baptist Gospel community.

These cultural traits dug from the depth of the soul of these displaced African populations tend to be implicit but the exteriorisation or manifestation of such traits through practical steps generate a collective knowledge that becomes an acute function of such a collective consciousness. Such a mechanism of survival is linked to the various notions of instincts and intuition which are linked to the innate nature of an intelligence expressed through the mechanism of creativity reflected in the arts.

Creativity in displaced populations represents the vehicle through which these traumatized West African populations exorcised their living conditions and as such what comes out of their collective soul is what is the most important to their sense of identity and/or innate aesthetics. It is accepted that in traumatized populations creativity is a natural force which through action is reflected in the dynamic expression of its arts and which standards of aesthetics are transferred through such media.

It is essential to realize that creativity through the Senghorian concept of rhythmic intuition generates an internal intuitive impulse of action first that comprehension will define second. The mechanism of intuitive knowledge first expressed in the arts and comprehension second is never better expressed than in the crystallization of these West African standards of aesthetics that give the United States of America its first sense of cultural identity away from the European canons of aesthetics through the emergence of the rural blues, the explosion of the Harlem Renaissance, and the Be Bop revolution implicitly dominated by a new sense of rhythm that extends to every media, through music, fashion, visual arts, poetry, literature, etc. ...

Senghor and Cesaire further state that West African populations share in a cultural concept or "Negritude" which is bound by two fundamental traits; the power of the image or metaphor and a visceral appreciation of rhythm and its sonic expression (Senghor, 1964). The notion of image and/or metaphor exemplifies the commonality of aesthetics of West African populations as expressed in their art, sculpture, paintings, where symbolism becomes an abstract expression of a power and/or a force that we feel but do not necessarily need to codify logically (Diagne, 2007). The great Afro Caribbean thinker Aime Cesaire states that in the African culture "the object does not signify what IS but rather what it SUGGESTS" thus giving life to the symbol by allowing for the freedom of interpretation as well as improvisation. Similarly, West African art or artistic expression does not signify what is but what it projects and what it suggests. West African culture functions in the acceptance and description of an abstract world through its arts but an abstract world where the forces of nature are given their full place and hierarchical status.

To Leopold Sedar Senghor, scholar, statesman, and poet, father of the socio-cultural concept of "Negritude", the concept of rhythm is attached to the image for it informs the metaphor in West African culture. Rhythm is the concept that articulates the notion of being, the quintessential relationship to life, and the internal visceral force that animates human beings. Senghor defines creativity through rhythm as the expression of "La Force Vitale" (Senghor, 1964). Senghorian philosophy states that to West Africans "*Rhythm is expressed in its most sensual lines, surfaces, colors, architectural volumes, sculptures, and paintings, accents in poetry, syncopation in music, motion and movement in dance, rhythms animates and informs all that comes from the revelation of being. Rhythm illuminates the Mind*" (Senghor, 1964).

Rhythm expressed in Mandinka Dancing

Rhythm expressed in the traditional style of clothing of this group of women.

Rhythm expressed in the design symmetry and choice of colors of the ceiling of the Keur Moussa abbey in Senegal

Rhythm expressed in the choice of design lines and expression of volumes in West African masks

In order to appreciate the role of creativity and intuition and the place these two concepts have as vehicles of socio-cultural change we must first understand that creativity as an intuitive impulse is not a function limited to our existence but it rather is an energy flow emanating from a Life Force that moves through all of us. The fact that we are able to feel a creative urge exemplifies the above stated notion that creativity and intuition are both visceral parts of a sub-conscious body of knowledge and that they may rise to the surface of our consciousness at any given time but particularly in times of great human trauma generated by deep sentiments of angst, sorrow, hopelessness, hope and/or love and/or lack thereof.

In his revolutionary work Henri Bergson (1907) states *that "any human endeavor, that involves inventing, any voluntary act that involves a sense of freedom of expression, any organism of expression that manifests spontaneity brings something new into the world"*, thus exemplifying the notion that we are by the very nature of our being part of a larger flow of intuitive force and subconscious knowledge.

It is important to note that in the case of these displaced West African populations to North America, creativity is boundless where comprehension and understanding of such intuitive impulses are bound to the finite nature of its end product i.e. Jazz, Swing, Bebop etc. … Swing as a West African intuitive rhythmic impulse derived from the concept of steady motion flow is an extension of an innate intuitive force that can only be felt to be appreciated but any attempt to write such a cosmic rhythmic phenomenon is restricted by the vocabulary of its translators, thus such an intuitive knowledge derived from a spectrum of space of vibrational dimensions cannot be described successfully in Cartesian terms, thus the need for the return to an African intuitive knowledge of rhythmic metaphor expressed through the symbol, the swing feel and its cosmic charge. This is defined by the infinitesimal appreciation of space between the snap.

Through the experience of trauma of these African populations we can appreciate that knowledge and action are linked to the intuitive nature of the individual and/or collective ability to transfer such an innate concept onto a media of sort be it a musical instrument for the musician, a brush for the painter, a mold for the sculptor, a rhythmic verse for the poet etc. … As such, in North America, the intuitive knowledge of West African standards of aesthetics by African populations is re-introduced and expressed through the mastery and disruption of understood norms and values of musical instruments, writing styles, compositional styles, approaches to fundamental elements etc. … Bergson (1907) states that *"there are things that only intelligence is capable of looking for but will never find and whose existence only intuition would identify but would never look for on its own."* Similarly, African Americans intuitively transferred through the creative process the notions of steady motion flow that animates the rhythmic syncopation patterns that colors all fields of African expression in any given media.

Rhythm expressed in the details of this mural on a wall in Dakar, Senegal, El Hadj Malick Sy, leader of the Mouride Sufi sect. (Mouhamadou Fadilou Mbacké)

B. WHY DO AFRICAN AMERICANS CLAP ON TWO AND FOUR AS MUSICAL NORM?

The verification that Senghorian, Cesairian and Bergsonian creative rhythmic intuition theories were at work in North America lays in the fact that African Americans fairly early on as they re-configure the songs of the Church of England through the evolutionary process of the African American Gospel Church will begin expressing the need to clap on the second (2) and fourth (4) beats of any given European musical system in which the

"The Old Plantation," South Carolina, about 1790

This famous painting shows Gullah slaves dancing and playing musical instruments derived from Africa. Scholars unaware of the Sierra Leone slave trade connection have interpreted the two female figures as performing a "scarf" dance. Sierra Leoneans can easily recognize that they are playing the shegureh, a women's instrument (rattle) characteristic of the Mande and neighboring ethnic groups. (Opala, 1986)

quarter note is the unit of count. While there does not seem to be a rationale for this most amazing phenomenon, given the fact that West Africans clap on one (1) at any given time and that Europeans also count one (1) as their referential time element the theory that we are advancing lays here;

We know that, through ancestral drumming sequences verified by oral tradition through the transfers of drum patterns from fathers to sons in the Kouyate, Diabate, Cissokhos Djali families of West Africa, West Africans mostly use one (1) as their referential element of time both as a rhythmic norm and a symbolical value and they conceptually physically, metaphysically and rhythmically oppose three to two,

We also know that West Africans clap on one (1) as a matter of cultural norm,

We know the importance in West Africa of keeping a steady rhythmic flow i.e. swing as a matter of cultural musical norm and metered value,

We know the importance of the concept of one (1) and its constant polyrhythmic opposing subdivisions as a matter of rhythmic referential value,

We know that the measure with a four (4/4) beat division sequence doesn't mean much when applied to West African rhythmic flow because it doesn't meet its polyrhthmic sequential patterns necessities and sensibilities,

So why would African Americans and the rest of the nation clap or accent two (2) and four (4) as a matter of cultural musical norm?

The answer lays in West Africa.

African American choir members expressing and clapping on 2 and 4

Djembe players from West Africa performing traditional rhythms

The creative rhythmic intuitive process for West Africans requires the physical expression of the subdivision of time of three (3) against two (2) (3/2) for any given referential rhythmic flow entity, six against four (6/4), six against eight (6/8), twelve against eight (12/8) which induces a feel that Ellington referred to as "Swing". This rhythmic intuitive process of time subdivision extends to the movement of the dancers that we can observe when we watch West Africans dance. Their movements gain amplitude because the subdivision of three takes place generating a feel of flow that is visually palpable. This need for rhythmic flow has been ancestrally expressed by the most popular West African 6/8 rhythm called Djembe rhythm and the drum that carries its name.

The Djembe drum is of Malinke origin (Mali) and is played throughout West Africa from Gambia to Nigeria which explains the depth of the cultural standards of aesthetics' reach of that instrument and the rhythm that bears its name, Djembe rhythm. The Djembe rhythm itself accents or syncopates the end of one (1) widely into the second (2) beat with an additional accent on the fourth (4) beat when counting a 6/8 pulse in a 4/4 meter system. In order to appreciate the sense of swing feel for two and four of the Djembe rhythm we need to count the 6/8 pulse in a 4/4 meter system and there we can observe the accents lasting on 2 from the triplet over 2 beats and on the fourth (4) while polyrhythmically playing 6/8.

Example:

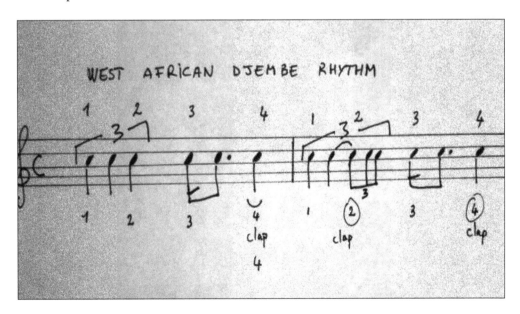

Africans in North America who were deprived of their drums by the slave owners intuitively re-created the ternary polyrhythmic subdivision of their ancestral Djembe drumming and sub-consciously and consciously extended its accents from the triplets over 2 beats on (2) two with the accent on the (4) fourth beat and applied it to any given form of music (4/4) included, thus forcing the integration of this aesthetic of polyrhythm and creating this powerful sense of swing which gave any music African Americans sung its unique African syncopated rhythmic identity that we witness during the worship services of the African American Baptist church.

The secret of the 2 and 4 rhythmic clapping of the African American community from the blues, to Gospel which gave birth to Jazz is in the intuitive rhythmic expression of the standards of aesthetics of the 6/8 feel of the syncopated Djembe Rhythm of Mali, its ternary subdivisions, and its accents.

C. THE ORAL TRADITION: INTRINSIC AFRICAN MODE OF TRANSMISSION OF KNOWLEDGE

Up until recently African societies functioned along the lines of the caste system in which a specific group of people provides goods or services for the benefit of the community at large. Empirical discoveries, trade secrets and the ability to maintain such trade secrets from other population groups remained the main mode of survival of such casts (blacksmiths, hunters, craftsmiths, healers, etc. …). As such the oral tradition became the best vehicle for guaranteeing secrecy, for one had to be initiated to obtain knowledge and only through this initiation process would one be determined by the elders whether he or she was worthy of such knowledge.

While Africans invented linear writing before the Greeks (Diop, 1960) and Africans were the first to write, the use of the oral tradition has remained a choice mode of transmission of knowledge. Initiation for worthiness of knowledge has always been a hallmark of African culture through secret societies, fraternities and sororities. We need to be reminded often that chronologically these West African societies moved their cultural practices from the area that was the Sahara and the West part of the African continent to Sudan first (Diop, 1963) and made their way to Egypt second (Davidson, 1982).

For people steeped in African culture and its quasi visceral attachment to the oral tradition principles it is not difficult to understand why we have never found the mathematical and physics theorems to build pyramids. These notions of secrecy and initiation tied to the concept of responsibility and honor as the sinequanone conditions for the transmission of higher spheres of knowledge explain why in our advanced age of technology we still don't know how to build such pyramids. The abstract mathematics, physics and architectural concepts of such testaments to Africa's great civilizational centers and technological prowess have continued to evade us at a time where we have been to the moon and back.

Africans believe that the absence of the availability of that information lays in the oral tradition transmission process of that knowledge so to safeguard it from foreign acquisition (Lubicz, 1938). The knowledge and understanding of abstract mathematics and physics that was required to build such pyramids that represented the apex of Egyptian civilization and their relationships to the Gods was the property of the great priests and that knowledge was most probably passed on orally as traditionally conducted in Africa through a complex set of initiations so that Barbarians could never get a hold of it, and they never did. Otherwise, one can be assured that the Greeks and the Romans would have built pyramids twice the size as those found in Egypt.

The high priests of Egypt were very mindful of Barbarian and Greek infiltration in their academia and Greek appropriation of Egyptian knowledge. Alexander the Great, who built his capital in Africa, in Alexandria and not in Greece or Macedonia once chastised Greeks scholars who claimed to have invented such and such theories. *"It would take a book of a thousand pages to name all of you who took knowledge from Egypt"* stated Alexander the Great (Freud, 1939).

It is interesting to note that for all the mathematical theorems depicting the laws of triangles carrying Greek names with inventors such as Pythagoras and others, there are no pyramids in Greece. The populations who actually used and applied such theorems namely the Egyptians and the populations of the Sudan testified of their understanding of such mathematical concepts through their architecture and the building of pyramids that have lasted the test of time.

D.   WEST AFRICAN VISUAL ARTS

There were great standards of aesthetics applied to visual arts in sub-Saharan Africa during the eras of the Empires of Ghana, Mali and Songhai and throughout the period of the Atlantic Slave Trade. These high standards of aesthetics touched every aspect of crafts-manship from jewelry, to sculpture, from painting to pottery, from rock art to personal decoration, from textiles to masks.

West African art offered an incredible variety of forms, practices, colors, and techniques that represented the diversity and the identities of the various ethnic groups represented on that part of the continent. West Africans expressed their religious beliefs, ritual practices, hopes, political aspirations, and standards of aesthetics through their visual arts with a high degree of technical mastery, coupled with an intuitive sense of rhythmic creativity and high abstract philosophical thinking (Diop, 1959).

The masters of African socio-cultural theories of aesthetics Leopold Sedar Senghor and Aime Cesaire (Senghor, 1964) express in the Book Liberte 1, Negritude and Humanisme that a metaphysical relationship exists between the African populations, their culture, and their innate intuitive expression and grasp of this phenomenon of rhythm. There is a sense of rhythmic syncopation and expression on and through all forms of artistic endeavours. This intuitive expression of rhythmic syncopation that we witness in African art extends not only to the movement in the dance and the sway in the walk, but also to the notion of volumes in sculpture, the lines in architecture, the choice of colors in paintings, the physical relationship to the instrument, the interplay of tones and the landscape of pitches, the production of musical forms and patterns that any object can infer and symbolizes through the African mind. This constant pervasive, cultural, intuitive and visceral relationship to the conceptual notion of rhythm and pulse has given the African mind its originality, its creativity, its strength but most importantly its identity.

The use of wrought-iron sculpture is specific to West African cultural groups such as the Dogons and Bamana people of Mali and Guinea, the Fon people of Dahomey (now Benin) and the Yoruba people of Nigeria. Between the 7th and the 16th century, West Africans used all the materials that were available to them such as wood for sculpture but also copper alloys, bronze, iron, ivory, pottery, unfired clay, and stone. The dynamics of lines, relationships of volumes, choices of material, patterns and colors are all indicative of the originality and individuality of these populations from West Africa who express through their understanding of rhythmic expression the conceptualizations of their metaphoric and symbolistic consciousness and sub-consciousness. Cesaire states *"that to Africans the purpose of creation is not to depict what IS but what it SUGGESTS"* (Cesaire, 1939).

The Empires of West Africa viewed the artwork of their smiths as elements of great cultural prestige and pride. Emperors, kings and wealthy patrons of the Empires of Ghana, Mali and Songhai financially supported their artists to excel because they understood how important the arts were to a sense of cultural identity thus the immense richness and variety exhibited in African art.

Bambara dance headdress of wood in the form of an antelope, representing the spirit Tyiwara, who introduced agriculture, from Mali. These headdresses, attached to a wickerwork cap, are worn by farmers who, at the time of planting and harvest, dance in imitation of leaping antelope.

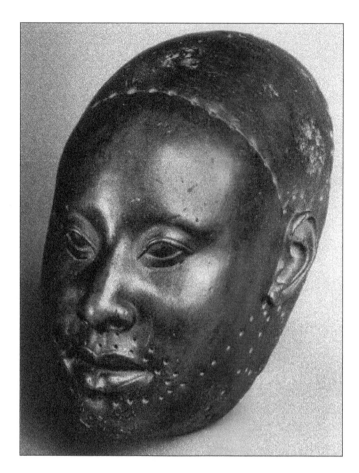

West African bronze head sculpture from the Yoruba, Ife, Nigeria, 12th century A.D.

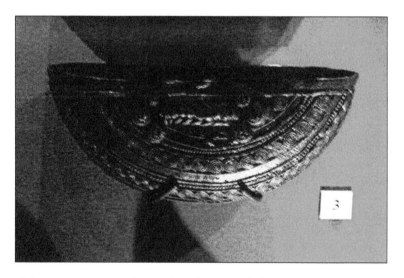

A bronze ceremonial vessel made around the 9th Century A.D., one of the bronzes found at Igbo Ukwu, Nigeria

Mali Terracotta horseman figure from 13th–15th century

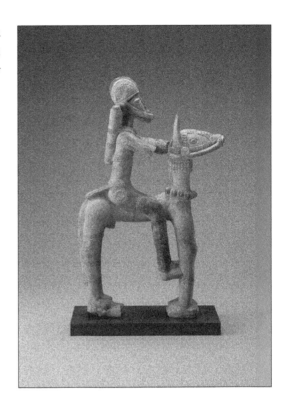

Terracotta Archer figure from Mali (13th–15th century)

Wooden stool, Dogon peoples, Mali, possibly late 19th to early 20th century. The Dogon describe the cosmos as two disks forming the sky and earth connected by a tree. The supporting figures represent the four pairs of nommo twins in their descent from sky to earth. (National Museum of African Art)

Wooden female figure Bamana peoples, Mali, Late 19th century, African Art Museum, Smithsonian

18th century Edo Peoples Copper alloy rooster, Benin kingdom court style. (Nigeria) Now in the National Museum of African Art, Washington, DC.

**Photograph of a pair of Ibeji twin figures, authenticated by the
Department of Antiquities of Nigeria**

Ashanti soul washer badge, or Afrafokonmu.18th century Ghana is part of an area that was a major source of gold for European and Islamic markets prior to the discovery of the metal in the Americas.

Kente weaving is a traditional craft among the Ashanti and Ewe people of Ghana. A kente cloth is sewn together from many narrow (about 10 cm wide) kente stripes. The picture shows 3 different typical Ewe kente stripes.

Wooden Yoruba Shango sculpture; Yoruba peoples, Oyo area, Nigeria. It is an emblem of Shango, the Yoruba God of Thunder.

**Wooden Door with lock, Workshop of Yalokone, Northern Senufo peoples of West
Africa. Wealthy and powerful individuals in the northern Senufo region commis-
sioned carved doors as symbols of prestige. The relief-carved motifs are associated
with the beliefs in the powers of divination, nature spirits and the supernatural held
by members of Poro, the men's initiation society that is found among a number of
groups in western Africa.**

E.   THE ROLE OF MUSIC IN TRADITIONAL WEST AFRICAN SOCIETIES ON THE BANKS OF THE NIGER RIVER

In West Africa, music as a medium and a discipline existed ancestrally and was passed on through an initiation process and with the consent of secret societies well before the chronicling of Ibn Batouta's memoirs of the XIIIth century and therefore before the existence of the term "Djalis" which appears in and around the XIIth century. To most West African societies, knowledge is understood to be in the sound which is conceptually short for sound wave vibrations. Africans conceptually and philosophically accept that the sound carry the power of the word or messages from the gods.

West African religious and philosophical rituals tend to use a specific sonic architecture, instrumentation and textures, rhythmic patterns and syncopation to construct and reveal the existentiality of their specific communal purposes within the context of their respective polytheistic paradigms as expressed in the various ceremonies of the Voodoo, or the Ndeupp, Bata, Palo and Abakua of Cuba, Candomble and Macumba of Brasil. Anchored in the mystical symbolism of religious disciplines, and ceremonies of the occult and magic, the worship of the deities and divinities, the acceptance of the various forces of nature as expression of the power of the gods that generate them and the still felt influence of the ancestors from beyond, music provides in West Africa the background and the communication tool to reach the depths of the above mentioned subject areas.

Through the daily rituals and songs outlining communal works and activities such as harvests, marriages, healing sessions, education of the youth, work and leisure, initiations, dances, storytelling of myths and legends, riddles, proverbs as well as wise sayings, names of people and caste systems, music provides a constant textural support to such cultural community activities.

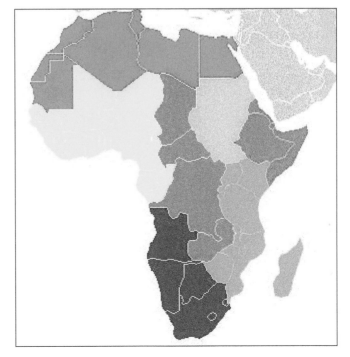

Geo-political map of Africa divided for ethnomusicological purposes showing commonality of standards of aesthetics. Alan P. Merriam, 1959

In West Africa, music in its tonal musical diversity and repertoire of songs also reflects the identity of the various societal casts such as those of the hunters, blacksmiths, herbalists, priests, mediums, whose activities provide community sustenance and social cohesion. The curative powers of music were evident very early on in Africa and the Diolas of the region of Casamance in Southern Senegal still practice sessions involving the use of specific drums tuned to specific tonalities to heal specific ailments such as epilepsy, seizures, nervous breakdowns, and various Casamance are called "Ndeupp".

There is a strong belief in West Africa that the power, production and dispensation of sound wave vibrations from a specific beat, for a specific period of time can re-align the centers of the human nervous system in a suffering individual. Similarly, the use of certain tones played by specific instruments can cause a loss of balance of that same human nervous system therefore there is a need for initiation into the nature of these specific findings hence the need for a caste system to preserve such a knowledge and its honorable usage. This knowledge has been safeguarded for centuries by West African secret societies (Butt-Thompson, 2003).

Induction into these secret societies only happens through an initiation process that is purposely painfully stringent so to deter amateurs, invaders or foreigners from joining. Whether we are referring to the Sande (women) societies of West Africa (Boone, 1986) or the Poro (men) societies, these secret societies are deeply indicative of the west African heritage of seclusion of specific information as they carry a tradition of secrecy

that involves the passing of cultural precepts, traits and traditions based on music and storytelling that binds these societies forever (Espie, 1967).

We do know that these secret societies journeyed to the New World through the slave trade as we witnessed the re-emergence of central West African musical and religious rituals in

A Kapsiki crab sorcerer of Rhumsiki, Extreme North Province, Cameroon, uses a form of divination by interpreting the changes in position of various objects as caused by a fresh-water crab.

the black communities of Cuba (Baataa), of Brasil (Santeria) and in the re-expression of the rituals of the Voodoo in the Caribbeans, Louisiana, Alabama and Georgia. Eric Charry (2000) talks about the significance accorded to a specific song *"Janjon"* from the musical repertoire of the cast of the Hunters of Mali as he describes the social requirements stipulated by such a cast to all those who wish to sing or dance to that specific song.

Music in West Africa did not wait for the induction of Djalis to play its cohesive role in the fabric of societies. The various casts (hunters, blacksmiths, fishermen, healers etc. …) around which West African societies articulated themselves from the beginning of the Soninke rule (5th century forward) had a musical repertoire that specifically addressed their identities, their histories, their genealogies, their accomplishments and successes and as such a code of secrecy was built around the notion that no music, or songs of significance to that cast could be passed on without an initiation process that would ensure its safeguard and survival.

A blacksmith of West Africa at work

Bozo fishermen of Mali on the Niger River, Mali

The Dogons of Mali exemplify the mystery and myth attached to these secret West African societies. Inhabiting the cliffs of the Bandiagar hills they refused to convert to Islam and have continued to practice the rituals and worships of ancestral African deities.

Dogon people of Mali

Ancient Dogon Cliff village near Bandiagara.

Dogon mask dance, music and percussions accompanying the rituals, Mali

CHAPTER 6

THE MUSIC OF WEST AFRICA AND THE CAST SYSTEM (JALIYA)

Music in West Africa infiltrates all social activities and represents an essential and integral part of society. A repertoire of songs accompanies all labor activities and specific songs are composed for specific kings, noblemen, and social events. Various caste systems such as the cast of the blacksmiths, the hunters, and the craftsmen have developed their own repertoire. Music is the vehicle through which the chronology of ancestry, the traditions, the glory and the challenges of a nation, but more importantly the history of great African kings is transmitted to new generations.

Djali is the Malinke word for the members of the cast of historians who hold the musical and oral tradition in West Africa in the land of Mande specifically. They are professionals who travel throughout the kingdoms and they are often assigned to work at the royal courts and serve the kings' emissaries. They are the repository of the history of West African kingdoms and they express this history through music and songs. They sing and play the balafon, the kora, and the ngoni primarily but also some percussion instruments.

Their cast is recognizable by the last names they carry such as, Kouyate, Diabate, and Cissokho. The Djalis claim that "Eh Jaliya, Allah le ka Jaliya da" or "God created the Art of the Griots." Their

Kora player Papa Diabaté from Guinea

art called Djaliya is a complex mix of music, history, genealogy, musical instrumental mastery, craftmanship, musical improvisational and socio-diplomatic skills. The Djalis are historians and scholars who know the chronology of West African kingdoms and cultural events. They belong to the three groups that dominate the Mande. The Bamanas located in central Mali, the Mandinkas in the eastern front of Mali and the Maninkas of the southern part of Mali. The Djalis are master intrumentalists and are also the craftsmen of their own musical instruments. They often look for the child, amongst the families belonging to their cast, who has "deugue" in Woloff which means the ability to hear a fixed tonality so that he can tune the instrument. This is what westerners call perfect pitch.

It is understood in African communities that if you cannot hear a select pitch as a member of your caste system, you cannot tune the instruments adequately, you can't build them competently and you cannot sell them effectively. The education of the Djalis is strict and starts at an early age, around 6 years old. They are required to master the various musical instruments used in the Djaliya. They have to learn the songs, the various instrumental accompaniments and the complex epic narratives of the Sunjata Keita era in particular. They must know the chronology of events, the names and ancestry of the various kings, clans and families of West Africa.

The Djalis are of particular interest to us because the bulk of the West African classical musical repertoire that defines the rules of harmony, melody and rhythmic patterns and pulse in West Africa that they sing, is anchored in the life and epic narratives of the 12th century Malian ruler Sunjata Keita. As such the Sunjata Keita repertoire and the use of its melodic tonalities, harmonic rules and rhythmic patterns that become the norm of West African musical sensibilities and artistic customs is responsible for shaping the

Djali Mamadou Diabate and the Kora

standards of aesthetics that West Africans taken in bondage will bring to the United States of America and particularly to the states of the South bordering the Mississippi Delta.

With the contemporary disintegration process of traditional socio-cultural structures in West Africa, Djalis are no longer employed by the kings' courts and find it difficult to survive. Their work today consists mostly of providing entertainment at baptisms, and traditional wedding ceremonies.

Master kora-maker Alieu Suso of the Gambia

A.   THE BALAFON

A Malinke term "Bala Fo" which means making the wood speak for this much celebrated instrument of West Africa.

The balafon is a West African instrument made of wooden keys strung over a frame with calabash resonators underneath. It is a fixed tonality percussion instrument. It is played by striking the wooden keys with mallets of various sizes. It usually counts 14 to 21 wooden keys.

In West Africa, the balafon appears in the 12th century epic narratives of the Malian warrior Sunjata Keita in his battle with Sosso King Sumanguru Kante at Kirina. The balafon was initially the property of King Sumanguru Kante. Clearly, the balafon is an instrument that existed prior to this 12th century epic story. After winning at Kirina, Sunjata Keita named Djali Bala Faseke Kouyate the guardian of the Souamoro Kante balafon. This sacred balafon instrument is kept at Niagassola in Guinea.

The tuning of the balafon is a more controversial topic of conversation. While most European classical music scholars recognize the pentatonic and heptatonic nature of the tuning of the balafon there is an academic reluctance to accept the diatonic sensibilities of the balafon tuning system for reasons that are unclear. A close study of the melodic lines of the Sunjata Keita musical repertoire sung by Djalis informs the listener of the unmistakably diatonic nature of these melodies. It bears logic that the diatonic melodic lines of that repertoire belong to the same tonal systems of the balafon which is the instrument of accompaniment of choice of the Djalis. Thus, the diatonic systems of tuning exist in West Africa around the 12th century at a time when Europe is still in the throngs of the five tone systems of the Gregorian chants. The balafon can also be paired in Djali ceremonies with the African harp or kora whose diatonic properties need no further testimony. This finding of the diatonic properties of the balafon was affirmed in my conversations with Dr. Yacine Badian-Kouyate, a descendant of Djali Bala Faseke Kouyate clan.

It should be added that all balafons are not equals. Some are made by youngsters to sell at the markets to westerners vacationing. Others are made to sell to other ethnic groups transiting through the area. However, there are specific balafons that are considered so sacred that they are reserved for special ceremonies. These balafons have special tunings and can only be played by trained and initiated cast members after certain purification rituals have been performed.

In the United States, the Virginia Gazette of 1776 (Southern, 1971) reported Africans slaves playing a barafoo instrument that looked like a balafon.

Balafon children from Burkina Fa

B.   THE NGONI

(The Ngoni, a plucked lute from West Africa)

Bassekou Kouyate and his ensemble

The Ngoni of the Malinkes is a lute and the ancestor of the American banjo or banjar (Jefferson, 1781). It is one of the revered instruments of the musical tradition of Mali and its age is believed to be anterior to that of the kora and the balafon. It is a popular instrument throughout the region of the empires of Ghana, Mali and Songhai. The name varies depending on the region of West Africa. Various ethnic groups give it various names throughout the region. The Malinkes call this lute ngoni, the Soninkes call it Xaalaam, the Diolas call it Akonting, and the Fula call it Molo.

The Gnawas who are people of Bambara descent living in the mountain of the Moroccan Atlas play a similar instrument called the sintir. This hollow body instrument with a fretless fingerboard comes in different sizes and most display 4 strings. The instrument requires the use of intricate fingering and plucking techniques involving a combination of strumming and percussive variations.

The ngoni like a lot of West African string instruments is often tuned differently based on the song or the repertoire. However, attention to the tuning reveals a consistent preference for the use of combinations of octaves, fifths and some variations of fourths. What is important to remember is that the rhythmic patterns and syncopation systems of the Malinke ngoni, which became the sintir of the Gnawa people of Morocco, are anchored in the polyrhythmic pulse of the three against two (3/2), six against four (6/4) and six against eight (6/8) steady motion flow concepts.

Given the fact that the instrument is fretless it provides the instrumentalist with a great variety of microtonal possibilities that is exemplified from one regional repertoire to another. The ngoni often accompanies the kora and the balafon and can be tuned pentatonic or heptatonic depending on the repertoire. In contemporary times, Banzumana Cissokho was the uncontested master of this West African instrument.

A Griot performs at Diffa, Niger, West Africa. Playing a Ngoni or Xaalam

Performer of the Diola ethnic group of Senegal playing the akounting

C.   THE KORA

Toumani Diabate, torch holder of the Mande traditions

The kora or African harp was introduced by the Mandinka group of the region of Mande. It is a traditional instrument of great harmonic and melodic range. It is a choice instrument of the Djalis of West Africa and its musical repertoire centers on the epic narratives of Malian Emperor Sunjata Keita. The current reigning master of the kora tradition and descendant of the Diabate Djali lineage Tumani Diabate confided to the San Jose Mercury News that he was the 71st generation of kora master (Gilbert, 2008), thus placing the kora in and around the 5th century.

The Scottish explorer Mungo Park describes the kora with 18 strings in 1799 (Park, 1816) as he travels the interior of West Africa. As depicted in the above picture its body is made from a calabash gourd cut in half and covered with an animal skin. The kora has typically 21 strings. Eleven strings on one side and ten on the other. In more contemporary times some Djalis have added extra low tonality strings. The tuning systems of the kora codify the rules of harmony and melody in West Africa. It is an instrument of soothing texture with ample range both melodically and harmonically. Its cascading and rippling notes gives the impression of listening to a stream of melodic pearls. In the past the strings were made of animal guts but in modern times they have been replaced by fishing lines.

**The kora—the African harp used by the Malinke
people of the Mande in West Africa**

The tuning of the strings tends to be in alternate of major thirds to minor thirds, F, A, C, E, G, B, etc., with some variation depending on the region where the instrument is played in Gambia or Guinea, for example. What is of note here, is the fact that the kora's age, its tuning and its repertoire leaves no doubt as to the diatonic relationship of its tonal systems, which would indicate that around the XIIth century, West Africans were using the major seven tones of their diatonic tonal systems. We also know that variations of the blue notes existed in the tuning of the kora depending on the regions of West Africa where the Djalis lived, Senegal, Gambia, Mali, Guinea, Niger, etc., But by and large the most common tuning was established in minor thirds and major thirds alternate.

The kora and the balafon are instruments that ancestrally have been performed in ensembles particularly in their expressions of the XIIth century Sunjata Keita repertoire and therefore there is no logical reason to continue denying the existence of diatonic systems of tuning in West Africa for the kora or the balafon. These West African diatonic tonal systems, dominant modes of harmony which make use of the blue notes in the musical repertoire of Sunjata Keita of the XIIth century are made evident in the songs of these ancestral melodies which are accompanied by the balafons, koras and ngonis. Listening to the songs of the Sunjata Keita repertoire one can easily appreciate the fact that these West African blue notes, tritones and variations of sevenths tonalities predate Baroque and Classical European cultural acceptance of such harmonic and melodic sensibilities.

We should point out that W.E. Ward in 1932 had already written about the intriguing notion that West African melodies carried the perfect diatonic scale in his article entitled

"Music of the Gold Coast" (Ward, 1932). The more interesting part of his article listed in the Musical Times, volume 73, number 1074, was the degree to which Ward conceded that African melodies in the Gold Coast sounded perfectly diatonic to a European ear yet he (Ward) could not accept that such ancestral African melodies could be the basis for the diatonic scale.

The importance of these findings explain why the music of the Delta Blues will be infused with West African "blue" tonalities, diatonic systems, dominant seven modes and the superimposition of the flatted third informing the revolutionary sharp nine harmonic function, most of which remains completely foreign to classically trained European ears until the end of the XIXth century but are present in West Africa and in the southern states of the United States of America where in some counties West African populations are the majority population (Horton 2004).

Jali Fily Sissokho, a Mandinka kora player from Senegal

D.   INSTRUMENTS RELATED TO THE KORA

Kamelen Ngoni

Griots musicians from Northern Sénégal (illustration de Côte occidentale d'Afrique du Colonel Frey) Kamelengoni from left, Ngonis right

Choice instrument of the West African hunters' societies of the Mande, the Donso Ngoni (6 string instrument) is the musical instrument used in traditional ceremonies for the accompaniment of epic narratives of Mali and Guinea oral tradition. The tuning of this instrument is usually pentatonic but choice local tunings were also developed. We also have the Simbi, and the Bolon who are related to the Kamelen Ngoni.

E.   PERCUSSIONS

Talking Drums

From West Africa this instrument is played throughout West Africa from Senegal to Nigeria. Performance requires technique with hand and stick, played by engaging the instrument under the arm and by exercising pressure on the strings pitch changes tonality from high to low.

Wolof *Tama* player, Yamar Thiam

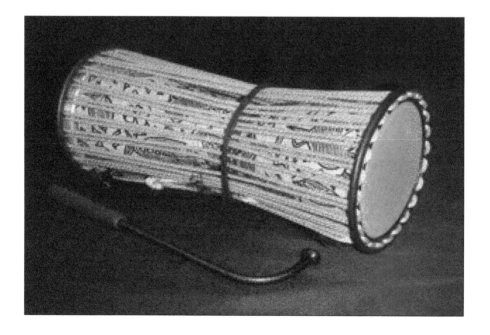

Bolokada Conde, djembe master drummer from Kissidougou, Guinea

Djembe

Djembes are hand drums of Malinke origins performed throughout West Africa from Mali, to Senegal, Guinea, Burkina Faso, Ivory Coast, Sierra Leone, Liberia, Gambia, Nigeria. This drum carries a rhythmic pattern that bears its name. The Djembe rhythm has a distinctive 6/8 pulse which when counted against 4 virtually expresses the 2 and 4 accents that generates the sense of swing heard in the clapping of the African American Gospel community.

Dunduns

The dundun drums are closely related to the djembes. They express the rhythmic patterns associated with low tones drums.

Three drums make up the dunduns set,
Largest and deepest is the dundunba,
Next largest is the sangban,
Smallest is the kenkeni. The dunduns are played with sticks.

Sabars

The sabar drum is the drum of choice of the Woloff ethnic group of Senegal. Seven drums make up the sabar ensemble set. They are the nder, the chol, the talmbat, the mbung mbung and the tungune. Each of these drums plays a polyrhythmic pattern to the overall sabar rhythmic pattern. The drumming technique requires stick and hand.

CHAPTER 7

❈

THE ATLANTIC SLAVE TRADE

A.   HISTORICAL PERSPECTIVE; SLAVERY AND THE ATLANTIC SLAVE TRADE

Slavery as a dynamic of human social interaction has seemingly been an ugly feature of human relationships from the dawn of times. The socio-cultural historical context of such interactions is present in the Old Testament. The Pharaohs of Egypt, the Assyrians, the Babylonians, the Greeks, and the Romans, the sultans of the Arabic Peninsula and Persia, the rulers of Asia, had slaves and managed economies based on the trade of humans from Asia, Africa and various parts of Europe.

The West African Empires of Ghana, Mali and Songhai are not immune from the historical plague of slavery and engaged in the commerce of humans resulting mostly from neighboring military conflicts that turned prisoners of wars into commodities. This was the reality of the political and economic life of these times. The main zones for such a commerce followed the trading routes of salt, gold, spices and crafts of the urban centers (Timbuktu, Gao, Djenne) of the Sub-Saharan and Saharan regions, to Europe, the Middle East, the Arabic Peninsula, and Asia minor through the Red Sea. It is estimated that nine million Africans were enslaved and departed through the trans-Sahara caravan routes and another four million Africans were traded through the Red Sea to Islamic ports. Four million Africans journeyed through the Eastern ports of the African coast. Zanzibar, a big center for the Arab slave trade and the Eastern seaboard of Africa through Tanzania remained an important contributor to the expression of this miserable human condition. Most estimates indicating how many Africans crossed the Atlantic through the slave trade tend to be conservative in nature and range anywhere between 12 and 20 million.

With the advent of the age of European exploration fueled by the tales of riches of gold and salt of these West African Empires, people of African descent were sold by African and Arabic traders to Portuguese and Spanish merchants in what is referred to as the first phase of the slave trade or the Atlantic Slave Trade. The second phase identifies more specifically the English, French, Spanish, Portuguese, Brazilian and Deutsch slave merchants. We should note that the medieval period related to the North-South economic relationship between the kingdoms of Africa and Europe, is not a time in the development of human social-interactions during which skin tone or skin color is necessarily a determinant factor associated with a defined social status. According to British scholar Basil Davidson *"racism based on skin color is in fact a rather modern disease"* (Davisdson, 1984).

European kingdoms were aware that the ruling empires of West Africa were governed by people of black skin, who were powerful militarily, wealthy economically, educated socially, and who administratively managed vast land areas of diverse population groups, while ensuring the safety of trade routes and flourishing urban centers (Davidson, 1984). Similarly white skin was not associated with education and sophistication in West Africa. Conversely, Europeans did not associate African black skin with poverty or illiteracy until the arrival of the firearm that will lead to the socio-cultural implosion and destabilization of West African kingdoms whose complicity allowed for the Atlantic Slave Trade to take place.

It should be noted that these three African Empires Ghana, Mali and Songhai were too strong militarily and too powerful economically for European empires to consider military options as a means to obtaining African slaves, as such the capture, sale and trade of slaves as commodities could only be organized from within the African continent. African merchants and Arab merchants, who had social ties to the heads of the empires of these times, provided the connection for Europeans merchants to buy slaves on the continent.

The status of slaves in most West African societies usually meant the equivalent of indentured servitude. The main reason for this distinctive status of slave as an integral part of West African society and family structure had to do with the fact that West African kingdoms did not have prison systems in which to house prisoners of wars. Prisoners of wars became slaves, and there was a military code of honor that stipulated that running away was futile. Consequently slaves received wages for their labor and were allowed to own property. In medieval Africa, the socio-economic status of slaves in West African societies did not prohibit the individual from attaining leadership and respectable positions of power in such societies. I have witnessed this much in my own family structure in Segou, Mali.

Built by European merchants large trade centers and forts were situated on the "Wind Coast" (the Gambia, Guinea), on the "Seed Coast" (Sierra Leone, Guinea), the "Ivory Coast", the "Gold Coast" (Ghana, Togo), the "Slave Coast" (Benin, Nigeria, Cameroon and Gabon) and on the Angola coast line (the Congo, Angola). During the16th through the

Reproduction of a handbill advertising a slave auction in Charleston, South Carolina in 1769.

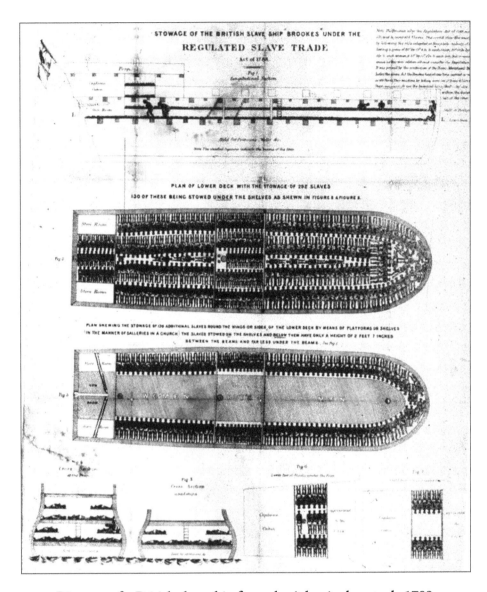

Diagram of a British slave ship from the Atlantic slave trade 1789.

19th centuries the Atlantic slave trade was concentrated on these specific coastal shores. It is culturally significant because these shores of contemporary Gambia, Guinea, Ivory Coast, Ghana, Liberia, Sierra Leone, Togo, Burkina Faso, Cameroon, Benin, and Nigeria along with the states on the banks of the Niger River represent a geographical area which has been infused with the civilization, the languages, the commerce, the rituals, the beliefs, therefore the standards of aesthetics, thus the music of the Empires of Ghana, Mali and Songhai for a period approximating fifteen centuries.

While historical data seems to indicate that the slave trade lasted three and a half centuries, unreliable documentation has made it difficult to accurately quantify the magnitude of this human catastrophe in West Africa. However, there seems to be academic agreement that between 9.5 and 12 million Africans arrived to the New World (Horton, 2004). From the mid 17th century forward the Portuguese, Spanish, French, English, Scottish, Brandenburg-Prussian Danish, and Dutch governments and slave trade merchants competed and intensified their human trafficking with the Kingdoms of Fouta Tooro, and Jolof, the Kingdoms of Khasso and Saalum of Senegal, the Kaabu Empire of Guinea Bissau, the Kingdom of Fouta Djallon of Guinea, the Koya Temne of Sierra Leone, the Kong Empire and Gyaaman Kingdom of Ivory Coast, the Bamana of Mande, the Asante Confederacy and Mankessim Kingdoms of Ghana, the Kingdom of Dahomey of Benin, the Oyo Empire, and the Aro Confederacy of Nigeria, the Bamun and Mandara Kingdoms of Cameroon, the Kingdom of Orungu of Gabon and the Kingdoms of Loango and Tio of contemporary Congo.

These Middle Passage voyages were dangerous for all parties involved. Africans would die of malnutrition, unsanitary spaces and diseases from the abominable travel conditions and ship captains and their crews could be killed by slave uprisings. Many ships fell under the direction of African slaves who killed the crews but did not know how to navigate back to their lands. We should note that in the French archives of the City of Bordeaux there are footnotes from French slave merchants who warn ship captains from mixing specific ethnic groups on the ship for these populations are known to be able to communicate and foment mutinies.

Death of Capt. Ferrer, the Captain of the Amistad, July, 1839.

Don Jose Ruiz and Don Pedro Montez, of the Island of Cuba, having purchased fifty-three slaves at Havana, recently imported from Africa, put them on board the Amistad, Capt. Ferrer, in order to transport them to Principe, another port on the Island of Cuba. After being out from Havana about four days, the African captives on board, in order to obtain their freedom, and return to Africa, armed themselves with cane knives, and rose upon the Captain and crew of the vessel. Capt. Ferrer and the cook of the vessel were killed; two of the crew escaped; Ruiz and Montez were made prisoners.

1840 drawing of the mutiny on the Amistad

Let us not forget the incredible presentation delivered by the former President of the United States John Quincy Adams before the U.S. Supreme Court in the spring of 1841 that led to the return of Cinque and other Africans captured in the Amistad (Jones, 1987).

It is with the support and complicity of West African rulers and traders, the encouragements and the funding of the European nobility, the assistance of European governments and merchants, the conspicuous silence of most religious communities, the economic aspirations of New World plantation owners, and the technological skills of shipping companies that we see a convergence of interests for the benefit of greed and lust for power manifesting itself into one of the most shameful human exploitation periods of epic proportion in the history of mankind.

B.   THE ECONOMICS OF THE SLAVE TRADE

Scholars have argued that profits from the business of slavery itself and that of the agricultural sector of the colonial plantations were the reasons for the successful funding of the economic growth and technological advancement of England, France, Portugal, Holland, and Spain prior to the Victorian era. Others have argued over the percentages of profits that the enslavement of Africans who produced the colonial economies of sugar, coffee, tobacco and cotton brought in. There is little doubt however that all these factors combined accelerated the development of technological innovations such as the steam engine that in turn played a paramount role in the development of the industrial revolution of the Victorian era.

While there continues to be a debate over the accuracy of the benefits European nations and the Americas extracted from the Atlantic Slave trade, it is clear to any reasonable student of history that three hundred and fifty years of free and applied human labor would generate an economic engine that would make any nation or nations on Earth wealthy for a significant period of time. Thus, the economic wealth of the United States, along with the riches of the colonies of the British, French, Portuguese, Spanish and Dutch empires were generated by West Africans brought to the New World for the sole purpose of forced labor.

The argument regarding the importance of the contributions of free African labor plays into the economic strength of the States of the South of the United States and is made evident as it informs later the divergent economic interests that begin to create friction between the Southern and Northern States of the Union which will lead to the American Civil War of 1861–1865.

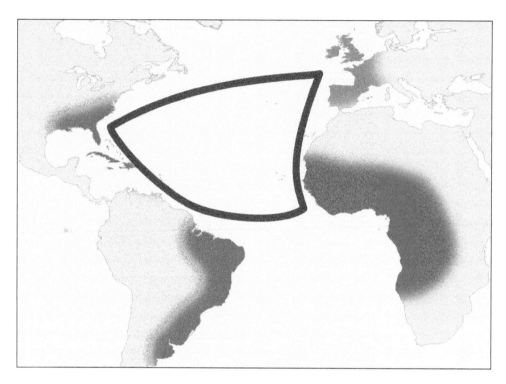

Golden Triangle—Europe, Africa, the Americas
Commercial goods from Europe were shipped to Africa for sale and trade for enslaved Africans. Africans were in turn brought to the regions depicted in blue, in what became known as the "Middle Passage". African slaves were thereafter traded for raw materials, which were returned to Europe to complete the "Triangular Trade".

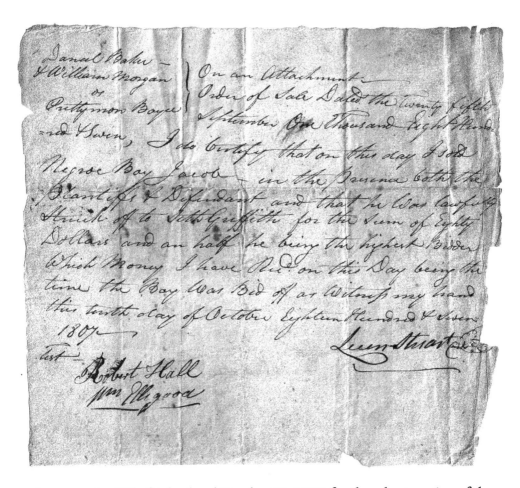

A manuscript Bill of Sale, dated October 10, 1807, for the sale at auction of the
"Negro Boy Jacob" to Seth Griffith, the high bidder, for $80.50 in partial settlement
of a money judgment against Prettyman Boyce, defendant, whose "property" Jacob
had previously been.
The Cooper Collection of U.S. Historical Documents

Atlanta, 1864. A slave auction house on Whitehall Street, Atlanta, in fall 1864, before it was burned by Sherman's army in 1864. *Library of Congress, Prints and Photographs Division*

Atlanta, 1864. A slave auction house on Whitehall Street, Atlanta, in fall 1864, before it was burned by Sherman's army in 1864. *Library of Congress, Prints and Photographs Division*

James Hopkinson's Plantation. Group going to field. African American men, women and children stand around and in a horse-drawn cart. Edisto Island, South Carolina, 1862/1863. *Library of Congress*

CHAPTER 8

RHYTHMIC INTUITIVE CREATIVITY: THE BLUES

A. FUNDAMENTAL EXPRESSION OF WEST AFRICAN STANDARDS OF TONAL AND RHYTHMIC AESTHETICS AS A NECESSARY MEANS OF SURVIVAL AND VEHICLE FOR IDENTITY

From the Niger River to the Mississippi Delta, as West Africans transplanted from various parts of their West African kingdoms to the colonies of the South of the United States bound by an atrocious shared destiny begin the process of forming the foundations of a common culture, a new music drawing from the depth of their West African cultural traditions, creative intuition and sensibilities emerges. These African traditions and intuitive techniques and expressions will inform the melodies and rhythmic cadences of the fieldhollers and the wordksongs, the harmonic rules and rhythmic patterns of the banjos, the sliding blue and bent notes of vocal expressions of joy and sorrow, the re-conceptualization of the hymns of the Church of England, and the social crystallization of expressing pulse by snapping or clapping on beats two and four as a manifestation of a polyrhthmic synergy of three against two (quarter note triplets over two beats) which gave birth to what we call "the swing feel". This emerging music from the depths of the intuitive creativity of these African populations located throughout the Southern states and around the Mississippi Delta will later be termed *"the Blues"*.

The Blues as an instrumental form of music communicates vocally and instrumentally the expression of standards of aesthetics born out of the musical traditions of West Africa based on singular

West African musicians playing the sabar drum

rhythmic patterns, blue note sequences, bent notes and improvisational freestylings. The Blues emerges as the bonding cultural form of musical expression of African-American communities that truly depicts the socio-cultural experience of black people in North America. These musical traditions that informed and shaped the shouts, the chants, the fieldhollers, the worksongs transformed the hymns of the Church of England into Negro Spirituals to give birth to Gospel or the music of the African American Baptist Church draw their standards of aesthetics or expression from the centuries old cultural legacies of the communities located on the banks of the Niger River.

While the origins of the term Blues as a specific referential term for the music of the Mississippi Delta are unclear, some scholars indicate that the term Blues was connected to the color of the devil which in XVI century England was blue. Others claim that some African groups might have been brought over specifically for their knowledge of indigo cultivation and processing (Rembert, 1979) which would dye their skins and fingers blue or their abilities to grow rice. We do know that West African ethnic groups such as the Touaregs, Songhai, Malinkes, Dogons, Yorubas and Hausas had used indigo for their clothing as early as the 11th century.

While there is an academic fog around the exact origins of the term Blues, the freestylings of the early Blues evoke without a doubt the great musical traditions of storytelling of the people issued from Mande civilizations and traditions. The Blues became the choice harmonic, melodic and rhythmic vehicle of expression of the despair, hopes and aspirations of Africans in North America. Although the Blues gained an association with maltreatment, oppression and misery, there has been a misconception that the Blues were exclusively sad since the music was an intrinsic expression of the socio-cultural experience of West Africans in North America.

In fact, it was the civilizational strength of the Empires of Ghana, Mali and Songhai that gave these various West African ethnic societies transported to North America the ability to recreate through music a bonding cultural element as well as a vocabulary for the expression of their common socio-cultural experience in the United States.

West African musician playing the ngoni

These transferred West African musical standards of aesthetics became the social syner-gistic elements that allowed these various ethnic groups from West Africa to come together as a community in the United States and absorb new influences. While the music of West Africans on the plantations certainly reflected the abysmal depth of the unimaginable pain and social horror of these enslaved communities, West Africans never stopped hoping for a brighter day. Their music in the early rural Blues also reflected such optimism. The reverend Wyatt reflects that sentiment when he stated that *"Music was the key ingredient that bonded black life together as a surviving people in North America" (Walker, 1986).*

The early Blues were singular and intriguing since they did not necessarily reflect a need for metric exactitude and the accompaniment followed the imagination of the storyteller. The manipulation of the harmonic seventh interval in instrumental and vocal expressions of African Americans is characteristic of the music of the Mande and resurfaces in the music of the Mississippi Delta Blues.

Scholars in the field of ethnomusicology are aware that steady motion flow tempos or notions of groove in 6 against 8 polyrhythmic patterns foundation along with the 7:4 tonality ratio were not features of Western classical musical canons. In addition, the introduction of the minor third at the octave in a major scale system or sharp nine is a West African concept that is supported by the ancestral tunings of the kora and the melodies of the Sunjata Keita repertoire as early as the XIIth century. These harmonic rules conceptually transferred into the socio-cultural lives of the African populations of the South and can be heard in the tonalities of the early recordings of the rural blues.

B.   THE MISSISSIPPI DELTA BLUES

Often considered the birthplace of the Blues, the African communities of the Mississippi Delta gave birth to a musical style that linked the West African musical traditions of the Empires of Mande expressed intuitively to the work songs and field hollers of slaves on Southern plantations. The chronology of the history of the blues predates the Civil War and finds its roots in the music, harmonies, melodies and rhythms of the African com-munities who lived on the banks of the Niger River of West Africa from which Africans in bondage in the United States themselves were issued.

It is understood that given the cultural magnificence and the longevity (1200 years) of the Empires of Ghana, Mali and Songhai, the Africans who came to North America brought with them the cultural traditions of their homelands. In North America, the percussions had been taken away from the Africans by the slave masters who realized then that Africans used them to communicate amongst themselves in effective ways. Slave masters in North America understood early on that the African drums only anchored deeper the socio-cultural bonds of Africans and the survival of their ancestral customs and beliefs. As such, the percussions were taken away and disappeared from the textures of North American music.

With limited resources to express their music, Africans in bondage in North America went back to ancestral techniques in which they used their voices as instruments, accompanied by hand-clapping as percussions. As a result of these converging socio-cultural and political situations, Africans in the Southern plantations of North America put together a style of music that expressed the foundational storytelling and musical forms of the Djali traditions of the Mande that we now call the Delta blues. The banjo whose ancestor is the ngoni, along with the jugs, bottlenecks, various forms of guitars and later the harmonica began to make contributions to the tonal colours, and bent pitches of this music which is as North American in its textures, as it is profoundly West African in its sonic, melodic and harmonic architecture. The logical place to begin this intuitive process of insertion of West African standards of aesthetics was in the re-engineering of the hymns of the Church of England and the creation of the Negro-spirituals.

African American Baptist Church, Silver Hill Plantation, Georgetown County, South Carolina

A river baptism in New Bern, North Carolina near the turn of the 20th century

Mahalia Jackson, photographed by Carl Van Vechten in 1962

The rhythmic expression of this need to infuse a sense of pulse through clapping in the music was also intuitively developed to accommodate deeply rooted African standards of aesthetics that required the conceptualization of rhythm as a counterbalance effect of three against two borne out of the ancestral rhythms of the Djembe. That is why in North America, African Americans snap on two and four. Snapping on two and four is the closest expression of the 6/8 feel born out of the djembe rhythm of West Africa, in an imposed European 4/4 meter, which led to this sense of pulse that America's foremost composer Ellington will later call "Swing".

West African dancing to djembes, gourds, and dunduns

18th-century painting, *The Old Plantation.* **African-Americans dance to banjo, gourds and percussions.**

In contrast, European classical musical standards of aesthetics actually prohibit musicians from marking the tempo using any body parts, whereas African musical standards of aesthetics require that you always mark the tempo with your foot, or your snap or your clap as an indicator that body, mind and souls are fully invested, connected and engaged. West Africans truly believe that if you can't tap while you are playing an instrument you can't play. To show how pervasive and influential African standards of aesthetics are in North American music, the person responsible for crystallizing a popular form of music (Hot Music) into an artform (Jazz), Louis Armstrong was quoted as saying that *"there are two types of musics, good music and bad music and good music is anything that you can tap your foot to"; he further stated, "I did not know what I was doing rhythmically until I went to Africa"* (Armstrong, 1956).

The blues, as it is now known, can be seen as a musical style based on the harmonic and melodic West African conventions of call-and-response, steady motion, flow, tempo concepts, blue note and bent note traditions, transformed into an interplay of voice and guitar that emulates the singing and communion of the Djali through his ngoni. A close listen to the melodies and riffs performed by the masters of Djali tradition of the Mande such as Bazoumana Cissokho reveals that the melodic patterns and rhythmic sequences that are the foundation of the early Blues come out of the standards of harmonic, melodic and rhythmic aesthetics of the civilizations of the West Coast of Africa. The fieldhollers, worksongs, and the early and rural blues are all informed of the West African standards of aesthetics of harmonic, melodic and rhythmic expression.

Elements such as the sequential systems of blue notes, pentatonic systems and bent notes can be traced back to the Music of West Africa. The early instruments of the Delta such as the balafon, the diddley bow, and the banjo are all African-originated instruments that played a significant role in the transfer of African standards of aesthetics related to performance techniques and vocal styles through the use of original melodic patterns found in West African music. These transfers shaped the fieldhollers, worksongs and the early blues vocabulary both instrumental and vocal.

The manipulation of the harmonic seventh interval in instrumental and vocal expressions of African Americans is characteristic of the music of the Mande and resurfaces in the music of the Mississippi Delta blues. The introduction of the minor third in a major scale system or sharp nine is a revolutionary concept born out of the expression of "hot music" first introduced on European battlefields through the music of African American Lieutenant James Reese Europe at the end of World War I.

Such tonal colors informed of the concept of blue notes born out of the African American quarters of the South of the United States begin a silent revolution in the minds of European composers such as Ravel, and Stravinsky in his 1919 *Piano-Rag Music* began absorbing and incorporating African American musical conceptual elements of the hot music of the red light district some called "Ragtime".

Anyone listening to the percussive styles of guitars of Son House or Bukka White, or the emotive vocalizing use of sliding tones of Robert Johnson and Charlie Patton combined with the rhythmic ideas grounded in the ancestral notions of steady tempo and rhythmic flow concepts, realizes that these standards of aesthetics are not coming from the music conservatories of Vienna, Austria or the Paris opera. These sounds are the intuitive West African standards of aesthetics as expressed vehicles for identity and survival mechanisms applied as a sonic reflection to the socio-cultural trauma experienced by Africans in North

1919 sheet music cover for "Good Night Angeline" with photo of composer and bandleader James Reese Europe and his famous 369th U.S. Infantry "Hell Fighters" Band who influenced Ravel and Stravinsky

America as a response to the Slave trade, lynchings, segregation, and the continuing cycle of economic, academic and political oppression.

The original lyrical form of the early blues that repeats several times and frequently takes the form of a loose narrative in a melodic and rhythmic pattern is consistent with the storytelling techniques of the West African Djalis as described by historian Leopold Sedar Senghor (Senghor, 1964). These musical phrases and lyrics are sung in a style that evokes a pattern closer to a rhythmic talk than a melody with the use of sliding tones or grace notes. Ethnomusicologist and guitarist Ry Cooder recognized this much in his travels to Timbuktu where he discovered Malian guitarist, vocalist, and farmer Ali Farka Toure in his village of Niafunke. The rhythmic, harmonic and melodic expressions of early blues artists Son House, Charley Patton, and Reverend Gary Davis have their roots in the ancestral rhythmic, harmonic and melodic standards of expression of Songhai Malian guitarist and vocalist Ali Farka Toure from Timbuktu.

Ali Farka Toure from Niafunke, Mali

John Lee Hooker performing live at the Long Beach Music Festival

In closing, when listening to the traditional music of West Africa, and that of Timbuktu in Mali in particular it becomes apparent that the standards of aesthetics of the culture and the music born out the West African civilizations located on the banks of the Niger River provided the foundational cultural and artistic elements for the expression of the distress and hopes of the black peoples of West Africa as they attempt to survive consciously and sub-consciously their common social experience in North America. From the depth of their intuitive creativity the emergence of a new music that will be termed Delta Blues begins to form. These tonal colors, rhythmic patterns and textures generate a sense of identity, worth and originality that links the African American experience to its ancestral fundamental musical principles which will in turn later inform America's only indigenous artform Jazz.

The sounds of the Mississippi Delta are deeply rooted in traditional African music and concepts and evolved through the social experience of African Americans in North America which will produce the Blues. The Irish populations who moved to the Tennessee valley in the 18th and 19th century found African Americans in the Appalachian Mountains who had been there centuries earlier and played the banjo, the jugs, the fifes, various homemade percussive instruments and sung the early rural blues. These newly immigrant Irish populations borrowed from these African American communities of the Tennessee valley the most African of instruments in North America i.e. the banjo as well as the sonic, textural, melodic and rhythmic architecture that they incorporated into their own folk music. Country music, which was born out of the rural Blues, also uses the banjo, and had its standards of aesthetics defined by an African American guitarist from Tennessee by the name of Leslie Riddle who collaborated with A.P. Carter and taught Mabelle Carter the guitar. The Carter family with Leslie Riddle helped introduce a new body of songs collected in the Appalachian Mountains around 1927 for Ralph Peer in what we refer to as the Bristol Sessions.

The African American guitarist Sylvester Weaver who defined the concept of slide guitar and gave country music its textural identity, died almost forgotten. Similarly, the inimitable harmonica player DeFord Bailey whose roots in the Blues objectified country music, was fired from the Grand Ole Opry because of a licensing conflict with BMI-ASCAP which prevented him from playing his best tunes on the radio, and spent the rest of his life shining shoes. African American Banjoists and fiddlers Horace Weston, Elmer Snowden, Odell Thompson, and Cliff Ervin remained unknown to most Americans despite their tremendous contributions to one of America's most popular music born out of the Blues.

Griots from Sambala, Mali, West Africa
(illustration de *Côte occidentale d'Afrique* du Colonel Frey)

African American musicians playing guitar on a tourist steamer in the South
Photo of the Okahumkee on the Ocklawaha, 1890s

C. MINSTRELSY A UNIQUE SOCIO-CULTURAL EXERCISE

Minstrelsy in the 19th century represents an amazing exercise in socio-cultural group behavior. As the nation struggles to find an identity of its own in the midst of its largest European immigration influx, newly arrived Europeans coming to the United States in search of a better life find themselves confronted to the reality that African Americans who have been here for 300 years have laid out for this nation a cultural and musical foundation that reflects its African standards of aesthetics.

Shocked by the lyrical and metaphorical depth of the Negro Spirituals, the rhythmic complexities of the syncopation patterns of the worksongs, the textural innovations of the instrumentation, the blue note intricacies of the melodic and harmonic systems of the musical culture of the African American communities of the South, European American artists desperate to survive financially, socially, intellectually and musically engage in one of the most ferocious counter-culture attacks in the history of mankind; the minstrelsy. The socio-cultural period of 19th century America in which European Americans, in an effort to further denigrate African Americans, discredit their contributions and deprecate their history, begin calling themselves Sambo, painting their faces black and drawing big white lips, is an ingenious, derogatory, and stereotypical cultural phenomenon and vehicle designed to rally newly arrived white immigrants and infuse them with a sense of social class and station against a common Negro cultural threat.

From the William H. West famous minstrel shows Billy Van (1882)

The cultural threat to European hegemony in the United States begins with the music of the African American community, thus the need for a concerted and coordinated effort to debase its progenitors and their contributions. This counter-cultural war is also a money-making venture of great significance, so much so that African Americans in an effort to put food on the table will paradoxically paint their faces black as well. European American owned minstrel companies are big business and travel worldwide spreading the derogatory stereotypes of the lazy, shuffling and illiterate black man who could never have contributed significantly to the foundation of a uniquely American culture.

Sheet music cover for "Dandy Jim from Caroline," featuring Dan Emmett (center) and the other Virginia Minstrels, c. 1844

Haverly's United Mastodon Minstrels

Blackface Virginia Minstrels in 1843,
featuring tambourine, fiddle, banjo and bones.

**Plantation scenarios of an 1875 poster for
Carrender's Colored Minstrels by Robert Toll**

**Detail from a playbill of the Bryant's Minstrels depicting the final part of the
walkaround, 19 December 1859. Scanned from *Dan Emmett and the Rise of Early
Negro Minstrelsy* by Hans Nathan**

CONCLUSION

Finally we recognize that the period between the 16th and the 19th century is the most important period in the development of an American indigenous architecture of standards of aesthetics articulated through music with the African and African American reconfiguration of the hymns of the Christian church through Gospel and the creation and advent of its secular cousin the Blues.

Between the 16th and the 19th century newly arrived Africans and African Americans in the south of the United States represented the majority populations in certain regional areas of the cotton belt and therefore the process of creating an architectural foundation for a unique culture began. These African and African American populations developed over a period of four centuries an identity defining musical vocabulary and language of their own that produce standards of aesthetics informed by their cultural and musical traditions from West Africa as well as the contemporary reality of the pain and horror of their socio-economic conditions in North America, hopes and aspirations.

We know that these plantation colonies were culturally separated from European influences, politically, technologically and therefore culturally. Politically, because European plantation owners despised the various kings and queens of Europe to whom they were to pay taxes, and culturally because they (plantation owners) fled Europe because most of them did not belong to the European ruling class of the times (Hester, 2000). We should note that between the 16th century and the 19th century there was little if any cross-cultural fertilization between Europe and the New World since technologies in the area of communications were nil and travel lengthy and dangerous.

Furthermore, in the absence of the technological revolutionary inventions of the turn of the 20th century, recordings and radio, European music of the time was stylistically anchored in the Baroque and Classical era, and provided no academic or intellectual support mechanism for the rhythmic, harmonic, and melodic rules that nurtured and informed the foundation of the music of the Mississippi Delta Blues.

The most important period of development for the emergence of American musical standards of aesthetics happens between the 16th and the 19th century for the nascent nation and its large African and African American populations of the South. These African populations who provide entertainment to the European American plantation owners are part and process in the South of the organizing of rhythmic, harmonic and melodic concepts that are anchored in African traditions and will forever color the hymns of the Christian church through the Negro-Spirituals of the Gospel.

While the most famous musician of Europe in the times of Mozart was a composer of African descent, the Chevalier de Saint George, Europe's premier violinist, fencer, colonel, and conductor of the largest orchestra of France, that of Queen Marie Antoinette, his incredible story remained submerged beneath the sands of time by European academia just like the socio-cultural contributions of the African peoples of the Empires of Ghana, Mali and Songhai whose men, women and children settled the New World.

Let us never forget that the stunning socio-cultural success of the degrading minstrel show era which featured African Americans, their music and its folklore was an effort by European Americans, in the mid 19th century period of the building of this nation, to discredit African Americans who had built a sonic, melodic, harmonic and rhythmic vocabulary away from European classical standards aesthetics for a nation that excluded them.

Lastly, anyone trying to point to the music of the Broadway shows of the early and mid-20th century as proof of European contributions to the development of American popular music and Jazz, should be reminded that the conceptual innovational bedrock of American music is founded on the intuitive concepts of improvisation, call and response systems, rhythmic syncopations, polyrhythmic expressions of time, bent notes, textural colors of the banjo, along with the chordal harmonies and melodies of West Africa which were long rejected by European canons because of the generation of blue notes considered devil's notes by the Christian Church, notes, rhythmic expressions and tonal colors so essential to the identity of the music of Ghana, Mali, Songhai and that of the Mississippi Delta.

And yet, it is these innovative West African tonal and rhythmic singularities that uniquely animate and inform the peerless identity of our American music through the Negro Spirituals, the Gospel of the African American Baptist Church and the Blues.

Portrait of the Chevalier de Saint-Georges by William Ward and Mather Brown
(Most famous Classical musician of the 18th century, violinist, composer, fencer and
savior of the first French Republic who influenced Mozart)

Musician of the Diola ethnic group of Senegal performing on the akounting

African American performing on the banjo

AFRICAN SOCIAL THEORISTS

<u>**Leopold Sedar Senghor**</u>

**Statesman, professor, writer and social theorist from Senegal,
founder of the concept of "Negritude"**

<u>Dr. Louis Leakey</u>

**Scientist and archeologist from Kenya,
demonstrated that human life began in Africa**

Aime Cesaire

Professor, and social theorist co-founder of the concept of "Negritude" from Martinique, French Caribbean

Basil Davidson

Professor, journalist, social theorist from Great Britain, provided a colossal body of research about African civilizations pre and post colonial times

Cheikh Anta Diop

Professor, scientist & social theorist from Senegal, demonstrated that Greek civilization was born out of Sudanese and Egyptian thought and culture

Dr. Ali Mazrui

Professor and Social Theorist from Kenya, father of the concept of the African Triple Heritage

Bibliography

Abraham, Arthur. Mende Government and Politics under Colonial Rule, Freetown, Sierra Leone Univ. Press, 1978

Abu Abdullah al-Bakri (1068) Book of Roads and Kingdoms or Book of Highways and Kingdoms (Arabic: كتاب المسالك والممالك, Kitāb al-Masālik wa'l-Mamālik)

Ajayi, Ade, J.F. & Espie , Ian, *A Thousand Years of West African History*, Great Britain, University of Ibadan, 1967.

Ajayi, J.F. and Espie, I. "Thousand Years of West African History" (Ibadan: Ibadan University Press, 1967

Armstrong, Louis, CBS Ghana, United Artists Video

Bakri, El, (1068) Description de l'Afrique Septentrionale, Mac Guckin de Slane, (1913) Jourdan, Paris,

Basil Davidson, *Black mother: Africa and the Atlantic slave trade* Harmondsworth: Penguin Books, 1980

Bergson, Henri, (1907) *Evolution Creatrice*, Presses Universitaires, Paris

Boone, Sylvia A. *Radiance from the Waters: Ideals of Feminine Beauty in Mende Art.* (Yale Publications in the History of Art 34). New Haven: Yale University Press, 1986

Boone, Sylvia A. *Radiance from the Waters: Ideals of Feminine Beauty in Mende Art.* (Yale Publications in the History of Art 34. New Haven: Yale University Press, 1986.

Bortolot, Alexander Ives. "The Bamana Ségou State". In *Heilbrunn Timeline of Art History.* New York: The Metropolitan Museum of Art, 2000

Caillié, René (1830), Travels through Central Africa to Timbuctoo; and across the Great Desert, to Morocco, performed in the years 1824-1828 (2 Vols), London: Colburn & Bentley Google books

Césaire, Aimé. (1939) *Cahier d'un retour au pays natal,* Paris:

Daniel Chu and Elliot Skinner (1992) "A Glorious Age in Africa," Africa World Press

David H. Rembert, Jr., "The Indigo of Commerce in Colonial North America," *Economic Botany*, 33 (1979)

Davidson, Basil (1984) "Africa" Video Series

Davidson, Basil (1998) "West Africa before the Colonial Era," Longman, Addison Wesley, London, 1998

Diabate Toumani, Article, San Jose Mercury News, Andrew Gilbert 2008

Diagne, S. B. (2007) Leopold Sedar Senghor; African Art as Philosophy, Paris, Riveneuve Ed.

Diop, Cheikh Anta (1959) *L' unité culturelle de l' Afrique noire: domaines du patriarcat et du matriarcat dans l' antiquité classique,* Paris: Présence Africaine.

Economic Botany, Volume 33, Number 2, 128-134, DOI: 10.1007/BF02858281

Eric Charry. *Mande Music: Traditional and Modern Music of the Maninka and Mandinka of Western Africa.* Chicago Studies in Ethnomusicology University Of Chicago Press (2000)

Freud, S. (1939), *Moses & Monotheism,* Vintage Books, Knoppf Random House, NY.

F W Butt-Thompson (2003), *West African Secret Societies*,. Kessinger Publishing

Gibb, H.A.R.; Beckingham, C.F. trans. and eds. (1958, 1962, 1971, 1994, 2000), The Travels of Ibn Battūta, A.D. 1325–1354

Gibb, H.A.R. translator and editor (1929), Ibn Battuta, Travels in Asia and Africa 1325-1354, London: Routledge

Hester, Karlton, (2000) From Africa to Afrocentric Innovations, 2002

Horton James, Horton Lois, (2004) Slavery and the Making of America, Oxford University Press

Insoll, Timothy (2003). *The Archaeology of Islam in Sub-Saharan Africa*. Cambridge: Cambridge University Press,

Jones, Howard (1987). *Mutiny on the Amistad: The Saga of a Slave Revolt and Its Impact on American Abolition, Law, and Diplomacy.* New York: Oxford University Press

Mazrui, Ali. 1986: *The Africans: A Triple Heritage* (New York: Little Brown and Co., and London: BBC)

Opala, J. "Sierra Leone: the Gullah Connection." (interview) *West Africa*, May 19, 1986, 1046–1048.

Park, Mungo (1816). *Travels in the Interior Districts of Africa: Performed in the Years 1795, 1796, and 1797.* London: John Murray.

Person, Y. (1963) "Les Ancetres de Samori", Cahiers d'Etudes Africaines (13), Paris

Schwaller de Lubicz, (1998) The Temple of Man, Apet of the South at Luxor, Inner Traditions, Rochester, VT

Senghor, Leopold, (1964) Liberte 1, Negritude et Humanisme, 1964, Edition Seuil Paris

Sigmund Freud, (1939) Moses and Monotheism,

Southern, Eileen (1997) [1971]. *The Music of Black Americans: A history* (3 ed.). W. W. Norton & Company

Stride, G.T. & C. Ifeka: "Peoples and Empires of West Africa: West Africa in History 1000-1800"

Stride, G.T. and Ifeca, C., *Peoples and Empires of West Africa.* Africana, 1971

The Indigo of Commerce in Colonial North America, David H. Rembert

Thornton, John. *Africa and Africans in the Making of the Atlantic World,* 1400–1800 Cambridge University Press, 1998

Walker, Tee Wyatt, Gospel Video, PBS, 1978

Ward, William E. 1932a. "Music of the Gold Coast." The Musical Times 73(1074): 707-710. ____1932b. "Music of the Gold Coast (Continued)." The Musical Times 73(1075): 797-799. ____1932c. "Music of the Gold Coast (Concluded)." *The Musical Times* 73(1076): 901-902

Wiener, Leo (1922) *Africa and the discovery of America* 1922.

Image Credits

Copyright © 2006 iStockphoto LP/Lise Gagne.

Copyright © 2010 iStockphoto LP/Nicholas Monu.

Copyright © JRPHOTO (CC BY-SA 3.0) at http://commons.wikimedia.org/wiki/File:Alexandra_Ansanel-li_in_Ondine_Royal_Ballet.jpg

Eric Draper, "West African Dance at the White House," http://commons.wikimedia.org/wiki/File:West_African_Dance_at_the_White_House,_2007Apr25.jpg. Copyright in the Public Domain.

Copyright © 2009 iStockphoto LP/redhumv.

James A. Bland, "Dancing On De Kitchen Floor," http://www.loc.gov/item/ihas.100004751/. Copyright in the Public Domain.

"UN Subregions of Africa," http://commons.wikimedia.org/wiki/File:Africa_map_regions.svg. Copyright in the Public Domain.

Copyright © Pmx (CC BY-SA 3.0) at http://commons.wikimedia.org/wiki/File:African_language_families_en.svg

Copyright © Luxo (CC BY-SA 3.0) at http://commons.wikimedia.org/wiki/File:Ghana_empire_map.png

Copyright © Roke (CC BY-SA 3.0) at http://commons.wikimedia.org/wiki/File:MALI_empire_map.PNG

Copyright © Roke (CC BY-SA 3.0) at http://commons.wikimedia.org/wiki/File:SONGHAI_empire_map.PNG

Copyright © jbach (CC BY-SA 2.0) at https://www.flickr.com/photos/51035624826@N01/736637307

Copyright © Olivierkeita (CC by 2.5) at http://commons.wikimedia.org/wiki/File:Balafon.jpg.

"Jeweler Gallo Thiam and the Kora Players," http://commons.wikimedia.org/wiki/File:Bijoutier_et_joueurs_de_kora.jpg. Copyright in the Public Domain.

Copyright © Richard Kaby (CC by 2.0) at http://www.flickr.com/photos/kabyric/2671252009/in/set-72157606187764055/.

Copyright © Schorle (CC BY-SA 3.0) at http://commons.wikimedia.org/wiki/File:Papa_diabate.jpg

Copyright © Tsui (CC BY-SA 3.0) at http://commons.wikimedia.org/wiki/File:Taj_Mahal_MQ2007-i.jpg

Copyright © Laytham (CC by 3.0) at http://commons.wikimedia.org/wiki/File:Honeyboy_Edwards_(blues_musician)_4.jpg.

Taharqa, "Mandinka Woman," http://commons.wikimedia.org/wiki/File:Mandinka.jpg. Copyright in the Public Domain.